Discover Your

SPIRITUAL GIFTS

C. PETER WAGNER

Regal

From Gospel Light
Ventura, California, U.S.A.

Published by Regal Books
From Gospel Light
Ventura, California, U.S.A.
Printed in the U.S.A.

Regal Books is a ministry of Gospel Light, an evangelical Christian publisher dedicated to serving the local church. We believe God's vision for Gospel Light is to provide church leaders with biblical, user-friendly materials that will help them evangelize, disciple and minister to children, youth and families.

It is our prayer that this Regal book will help you discover biblical truth for your own life and help you meet the needs of others. May God richly bless you.

For a free catalog of resources from Regal Books/Gospel Light, please call your Christian supplier or contact us at 1-800-4-GOSPEL *or* www.regalbooks.com.

Cover and Interior Design by Robert Williams
Edited by Rose Decaen

LIBRARY OF CONGRESS CATALOGING-IN-PUBLICATION DATA
Wagner, C. Peter.
    Discovering your spiritual gifts / C. Peter Wagner.
        p.   cm.
Includes bibliographical references.
    ISBN 0-8307-2955-0
    1. Gifts, Spiritual.   I. Title.
    BT767.3   .W33 2002
    234'.13—dc21   2001008735

1 2 3 4 5 6 7 8 9 10 11 12 13 14 15 16 17 18 19 / 09 08 07 06 05 04 03 02

Rights for publishing this book in other languages are contracted by Gospel Light Worldwide, the international nonprofit ministry of Gospel Light. Gospel Light Worldwide also provides publishing and technical assistance to the international publishers dedicated to producing Sunday School and Vacation Bible School curricula and books in the languages of the world. For additional information, visit www.gospellightworldwide.org; write to Gospel Light Worldwide, P.O. Box 3875, Ventura, CA 93006; or send an e-mail to info@gospellightworldwide.org.

CONTENTS

CHAPTER 1

A FAST TRACK FOR

Discovering Your

SPIRITUAL GIFTS

You may have heard of spiritual gifts. Most Christian believers have. Possibly you are among those who have identified your spiritual gifts and have been using them on a regular basis. But a surprising number of believers who have heard of spiritual gifts are not sure what theirs may be. And there are even some who feel that, for some reason, they have been left out and they do not have any of the gifts.

This book will help you understand that if you are sure you are a born-again member of the Body of Christ, you can be equally sure that you have one or more spiritual gifts. It will also set you on the road toward accurately identifying your gifts and then using them for their intended purposes. In fact, many readers will soon realize that they actually have been using one or more gifts without even recognizing that they are true spiritual gifts.

Once you start identifying your gifts, you will find that there are many excellent resources for helping you activate them. For example, my larger book on spiritual gifts has been circulating since the 1970s. But the fast-paced world in which we now live requires a smaller and more condensed manual like this one. Once you finish this, you may then wish to get the further details contained in *Your Spiritual Gifts Can Help Your Church Grow* or in many similar books.

Before going on, let me explain how the whole Body of Christ only recently woke up to the fact that God has given all of us one or more spiritual gifts.

REDISCOVERING OUR SPIRITUAL GIFTS

A relatively new thing happened to the Church of Jesus Christ in America during the decade of the 1970s. The third Person of the Trinity came into His own, so to speak. Yes, the Holy Spirit has always been there. Creeds, hymns and liturgies have attested to the central place of the Holy Spirit in orthodox Christian faith. Systematic theologies throughout the centuries have included sections on pneumatology, thus affirming the Holy Spirit's place in Christian thought.

But rarely, if ever, in the history of the Church has such a widespread interest in moving beyond creeds and theologies to a personal experience of the Holy Spirit in everyday life swept over the people of God to the degree we now see in our churches. One of the most prominent facets of this new experience of the Holy Spirit is the rediscovery of spiritual gifts. Why do I say "rediscovery"?

FIXING THE DATE

It is fairly easy to fix the date when this new interest in the Holy Spirit began. The production of literature itself is a reasonably accurate indicator. A decent seminary library will catalog more than 50 books on the subject of spiritual gifts. Probably over

90 percent of them will have been written after 1970. Previous to 1970, seminary graduates characteristically left their institutions knowing little or nothing about spiritual gifts. Now such a state of affairs would generally be regarded as a deficiency in ministerial training.

The Beginning

The roots of this new thing began in 1900, the most widely accepted date for what is now known as the classical Pentecostal movement. During a watchnight service beginning on December 31, 1900, and ending on what is technically the first day of the twentieth century, Charles Parham of Topeka, Kansas, laid his hands on Agnes Ozman, she began speaking in tongues, and the movement had begun. A fascinating chain of events led to the famous Los Angeles Azusa Street Revival, which began in 1906 under the ministry of William Seymour. And with that, the Pentecostal movement gained high visibility and a momentum that has never slackened.

The original intent of Pentecostal leaders was to influence the major Christian denominations from within, reminiscent of the early intentions of such leaders as Martin Luther and John Wesley. But just as Lutheranism was found incompatible with the Catholic Church in the sixteenth century and just as Methodism was found incompatible with the Anglican Church in the eighteenth century, Pentecostalism was considered incompatible with the mainline American churches in the early twentieth century. Thus, as others had done before them, Pentecostal leaders reluctantly found it necessary to establish new denominations where they could develop a lifestyle directly under the influence of the Holy Spirit in an atmosphere of freedom and mutual support. Such denominations that we know today as Assemblies of God, Pentecostal Holiness, Church of

God in Christ, Church of the Foursquare Gospel, Church of God (Cleveland, Tennessee) and many others were formed for that purpose.

The Second Phase

The second phase of this movement began after World War II when Pentecostal leaders set out to join the mainstream. The beginnings were slow. Some of the Pentecostal denominations began to gain "respectability" by affiliating with organizations such as the National Association of Evangelicals. Consequently they began to neutralize the opinion that Pentecostalism was a kind of false cult to be placed alongside Jehovah's Witnesses, Mormons and Spiritists.

In 1960, an Episcopal priest in Van Nuys, California, Dennis Bennett, shared with his congregation that he had experienced the Holy Spirit in the Pentecostal way, and what became known as the charismatic movement had its start. The charismatic movement took form first as renewal movements within major existing denominations, and then around 1970 the independent charismatic movement began with the emergence of freestanding charismatic churches separate from denominations. For the next 25 years, these independent charismatic churches were the fastest-growing group of churches in the United States.

The effect of all this soon began to be felt among Christians who were neither classical Pentecostals nor charismatics. Although many of these evangelical Christians still show little interest in experiencing the baptism in the Holy Spirit, the main distinguishing feature of these new movements is that they are appropriating the dynamic of spiritual gifts in a new and exciting way. Through their discovery of how the gifts of the Spirit were intended to operate in the Body of Christ, the Holy Spirit is now being transformed from abstract doctrine to dynamic experience across the board.

WITNESSING THE DEMISE OF CESSATIONISM

Not everyone agrees, however. Some who remain cool on spiritual gifts, for example, argue that many of the gifts went out of use in the churches after the age of the apostles. An intellectual center of this belief is found at Dallas Theological Seminary, an interdenominational school that has looked with disfavor on the Pentecostal/charismatic movement of recent decades.

John Walvoord, former president of Dallas Seminary, feels that miracles have declined in the Church since the age of the apostles. His colleague, Merrill Unger, makes reference to Benjamin B. Warfield of Princeton Seminary who, back in 1918, wrote a book called *Miracles: Yesterday and Today, True and False*. Other than the *Scofield Reference Bible*, it has been the most influential book written in America against the validity of the charismatic gifts today. Warfield argues that "these gifts were . . . distinctively the authentication of the Apostles. . . . Their function thus confined them to distinctively the Apostolic Church, and they necessarily passed away with it."[1]

The notion that the more spectacular spiritual gifts ceased with the apostolic age is now commonly known as cessationism. As I have detailed in my larger book *Your Spiritual Gifts Can Help Your Church Grow*, the charismatic gifts of the Holy Spirit have been recognized by relatively small segments of the Church from time to time throughout Church history. But until quite recently, cessationism has been the prevailing Church doctrine. Yet times are changing. Today, on a global scale, including the United States, most Church leaders would agree that cessationism now belongs on some "endangered doctrines" list.

REALIZING THE MINISTRY OF ALL BELIEVERS

Martin Luther permanently changed Christendom when he rediscovered the *priesthood* of all believers back in the sixteenth century. Still, Lutheranism retained much of the clericalism of the Roman Catholic Church. One wonders why it took more than 400 years for the churches born of the Reformation to rediscover the biblical teaching of the *ministry* of all believers. It is very important to understand the difference.

I believe that 1972 can be considered the year that the concept of the *ministry* of all believers attained a permanent status in contemporary Christianity. In 1972, Ray Stedman's book *Body Life* was published, and it became a best-seller. In his book, this highly respected non-Pentecostal leader recognized, in so many words, that spiritual gifts were OK. Although his list of the gifts turned out to be shorter than some others, because he also was a cessationist, Stedman showed clearly how spiritual gifts, the ministry of all believers and "Body life" had brought health, vitality and excitement to Peninsula Bible Church in Palo Alto, California.[2]

The ripple effects of the publication of *Body Life* have had a profound influence. Rare is the church today that will advocate that the professional pastor or staff should do all the ministry of the church. Although some have not been able to implement it as rapidly as others, most affirm, at least in theory, that laypeople should be empowered to discover their spiritual gifts and through them actually do the ministry of the church.

How this can become a reality in your life is what this book is all about.

Notes

1. Benjamin B. Warfield, *Miracles: Yesterday and Today, True and False* (Grand Rapids, MI: William B. Eerdmans Publishing Company, 1965), p. 6.
2. Ray C. Stedman, *Body Life* (Ventura, CA: Regal Books, 1972), n.p.

Being Everything
THAT GOD WANTS
YOU TO BE

One of the Scripture texts most frequently recommended to new Christians for memorization is Romans 12:1-2: "I beseech you therefore, brethren, by the mercies of God, that you present your bodies a living sacrifice, holy, acceptable to God, which is your reasonable service. And do not be conformed to this world, but be transformed by the renewing of your mind, that you may prove what is that good and acceptable and perfect will of God."

This Scripture goes on to say that the key to coming to practical terms with the will of God for our lives is to "think soberly" of ourselves (Rom. 12:3). This means that each of us needs a realistic self-evaluation as a starting point.

We need to take two steps—one positive and one negative—if we are going to "think soberly" of ourselves.

Negatively, we are not allowed to think more highly of ourselves than we ought to think. In evaluating ourselves, therefore, we have no room for pride. Sober judgments always involve humility.

Positively, we are to recognize that part of our spiritual constitution is a "measure of faith" (v. 3), which God has distributed to every Christian person. The implication is that every Christian may receive a different measure and, therefore, every Christian is unique. But unique in what sense? Before Paul answers this question, he gives us the analogy he is preparing to use extensively to explain spiritual gifts, namely, the analogy of the human body. "For as we have many members in one body, but all the members do not have the same function, so we, being many, are one body in Christ" (Rom. 12:4-5).

WHAT IS THE BODY OF CHRIST?

What, precisely, is the Body of Christ to which we have been introduced? Because the Bible says that we Christians are all one Body in Christ, we understand that it is a group of believers. It is the Church.

But how did God organize the Church, the Body of Christ?

On the one hand, God did not plan that the Body of Christ should be organized around the model of a dictatorship where just one person rules, benevolent as that person might be. On the other hand, neither did God intend that it should be a democracy where every member rules. This latter point needs to be emphasized, especially here in America where our civil culture prides itself so much on democracy and where this is frequently carried over into our churches.

Instead of a dictatorship or a democracy, God has chosen to make the Body of Christ a living *organism,* Jesus being the head and each member functioning with one or more spiritual gifts. Understanding spiritual gifts, then, is the foundational key to understanding the organization of the Church.

The major biblical passages on spiritual gifts reinforce the above conclusion. It cannot be mere coincidence that in all three of the explicit passages on spiritual gifts, Romans 12, 1 Corinthians 12 and Ephesians 4, the gifts are explained in the context of the

Body. "God has set the members, each one of them, in the body just as He pleased" (1 Cor. 12:18). This means that God has not only designed the Body on the model of an organism, but He has also gone so far as to determine what the function of each of the individual members should be.

If each one of us knows what our particular function is in the Body, we are able to "think soberly" of ourselves and launch into doing the will of God.

WHO HAS SPIRITUAL GIFTS?

Not everybody in the world has spiritual gifts. Unbelievers do not. But every Christian person who is committed to Jesus and truly a member of His Body has at least one gift and quite possibly more. The Bible says that every Christian has received a gift (see 1 Pet. 4:10) and that "the manifestation of the Spirit is given to each one for the profit of all" (1 Cor. 12:7). First Corinthians 12:18 stresses that *every one* of the members is placed in the Body according to God's design. Possession of one or more spiritual gifts is part of God's plan for every Christian.

This comes as good news to the average believer. It is pleasant to be reminded that God knows me, He loves me, and He considers me special enough to give me a personal gift so that I can serve Him. This is especially true in a society such as ours in America where many school districts establish special programs for "gifted children." The implication of that is that ordinary citizens aren't gifted. Not so in the Body of Christ! God gifts us all!

WHAT ARE GIFT-MIXES?

Many Christians are multigifted. I would suspect that probably the majority, or perhaps even all Christians, have what we could call a gift-mix, instead of a single gift.

Given the variety of spiritual gifts, the degrees of giftedness in each personal case and the multiple ministries through which each gift can be exercised, the combination of these qualities that each one of us has been given may be the most important factor in determining our spiritual personalities. Most of us are used to the idea that each person has his or her own personality. For example, my wife, Doris, and I have three daughters, all born of the same parents and raised in the same household, but each one of them is unique. God's children are similar. All Christians are unique members of the Body of Christ, and their individual identity is determined to a significant degree by the gift-mix that God has given them.

The health of the Church and its subsequent growth depend on this fact. I realize that it comes as a surprise to some Christians, who may have been only marginally active in church for years, to find out that they are actually needed, wanted and gifted to do their part in their local church. But it is true. In order for you to be everything that God wants you to be, there is no substitute for finding your gift-mix and knowing for sure that you are equipped to do the "good and acceptable and perfect will of God" (Rom. 12:2).

WHAT IS THE RELATIONSHIP BETWEEN GOD'S GIFTS AND GOD'S CALL?

Christians often speak of their calling. We frequently say things like "God has *called* me to do such and such" or "I don't believe God is *calling* me to do such and such." At this point, it is helpful to recognize that a person's call and his or her spiritual gifts are closely associated.

When related to doing God's will, your *general* call should be seen as equivalent to your spiritual gift. No better framework exists within which to interpret your call than to know your specific gift-mix. God does not give you gifts that He does not "call" you to use, nor does He "call" you to do something for Him without equipping you with the necessary gift or gifts to do it.

Besides the *general* calling, however, you will also have a more *specific* calling. Some like to refer to this specific call as a person's ministry. Your ministry is the particular way or the particular setting in which God wishes you to exercise the gift or gifts He has given you. For example, you can have the gift of teaching and be called specifically to use that gift among children; others may use the gift of teaching on the radio or in writing books. You can have the missionary gift and be called to use that gift in Zambia; others may be called to Paraguay or to Sri Lanka. Within the general calling provided by each gift, then, are many more specific ways that such a gift can be ministered.

WHAT IS A SPIRITUAL GIFT?

At this point, let's pause and define just what "spiritual gift" means. The working definition I like to use is as follows:

> A spiritual gift is a special attribute given by the Holy Spirit to every member of the Body of Christ, according to God's grace, for use within the context of the Body.

This is as tight a definition as I have been able to formulate and still retain what I consider to be the essential elements. Several of these elements, namely "special attribute," "given by the Holy Spirit" and "to every member of the Body of Christ" have been sufficiently discussed. Two other important phrases remain.

"According to God's grace" is a phrase that moves us into the biblical words themselves. The common Greek word for spiritual gift is *charisma*; the plural is *charismata*. Our contemporary terms "charismatic movement" and "charismatics" are derived from this Greek word. But note something else. "Charisma" comes from the root word *charis*, which in Greek means "grace." A close relationship exists, then, between spiritual gifts and the grace of God.

The final phrase of the definition, "for use within the context of the Body," reminds us that individual Christians disconnected from the Body are not very useful. Spiritual gifts are not designed for Lone Rangers. They are designed for members of the Body. Most of the things God does in the world today are done through believers who are working together in community, complementing each other with their gifts in their local congregations. It is important to clarify here, though, that this does not mean that gifts are always inward-looking and for the mutual benefit of Christians. In fact, many gifts are designed to benefit those who are not yet members of the Body.

ARE YOU READY TO DISCOVER, DEVELOP AND USE YOUR GIFT?

If spiritual gifts at work are a key to help you be all that God wants you to be, let's get practical. In light of the clear teaching of God's word, I think it is safe to say that one of the primary spiritual exercises for any Christian person is to discover, develop and use his or her spiritual gift. Other spiritual exercises may be equally as important, such as worship, prayer, reading God's Word, feeding the hungry, the sacraments or what have you. But I do not know of anything *more* important than discovering, developing and using your spiritual gifts.

Notice that I put "discovering" before "developing." This is because spiritual gifts are *received*, not *achieved*. God gives the gifts at His own discretion. First Corinthians 12:11 talks about the Spirit distributing gifts "to each one individually *as He wills*" (emphasis added). Later in verse 18 the text says that God sets the members in the Body *"just as He pleased"* (emphasis added). God has not entrusted to any human being the ability to give spiritual gifts. No pastor, no seminary president, not even the Pope himself is qualified to distribute spiritual gifts.

WHAT ARE THE BENEFITS OF SPIRITUAL GIFTS?

What happens if you do decide to discover, develop and use your spiritual gift or gifts? Several things.

First of all, you will be a better Christian and better able to allow God to make your life count for Him. People who know their gifts have a handle on their spiritual job description, so to speak. They find their place in the church with more ease.

Christian people who know their spiritual gifts tend to develop healthy self-esteem. This does not mean they "think of [themselves] more highly than [they] ought to think" (Rom. 12:3). They learn that no matter what their gift is, they are important to God and to the Body. The ear learns not to say "because I am not an eye, I am not of the body" (1 Cor. 12:16). Crippling inferiority complexes drop by the wayside when people begin to "think soberly" of themselves (Rom. 12:3).

Some are inhibited by a misguided idea of humility. They refuse to name their spiritual gift on the grounds that this would be arrogant and presumptuous on their part. This only exhibits their failure to understand the biblical teaching on gifts. Others may have a less noble motive for not wanting to be associated with a gift—they might not want to be held accountable for its use. In that case, appealing to humility can be used as a cover-up for disobedience.

Secondly, not only does knowing about spiritual gifts help individual Christians, but it also helps the Church as a whole. The Bible tells us that when spiritual gifts are in operation, the whole Body matures. It helps the Body to gain "the measure of the stature of the fullness of Christ" (Eph. 4:13).

The third and most important thing that knowing about spiritual gifts does is that it glorifies God. Peter advises Christians to use their spiritual gifts and then add the reason why: "That in all things God may be glorified through Jesus Christ, to whom belong the glory and the dominion forever and ever. Amen" (1 Pet. 4:11). What could be better than glorifying God? I agree with the *Westminster Shorter Catechism* which affirms that glorifying God is "the chief end of humans."

If using spiritual gifts helps me glorify God, I want to use my gifts! I know that you do also. It helps all of us be what God wants us to be!

CHAPTER 3

How Many GIFTS ARE THERE?

If we, the Body of Christ, the Church, function best with every member using the spiritual gifts he or she has been given, it becomes important to be able to identify the part that each member plays. We are a team. Good baseball teams, for example, understand perfectly the differing roles of a first baseman or a pitcher or a center fielder or a catcher or a third-base coach.

The parts of our human body all have names. God possibly chose the human body as the physical example of the Church because each human being, regardless of educational level, can accurately identify body parts. Everyone knows the position and function of a toe or an eyebrow or a lung or a hip or a tooth or whatever. We need to be just as familiar with the body parts of the Church, characterized by the spiritual gifts that God has distributed.

So, how many spiritual gifts are there, and what are they for?

OUTLINING THE THREE KEY LISTS

The great majority of the spiritual gifts mentioned in the Bible are found in three key chapters: Romans 12, 1 Corinthians 12 and Ephesians 4. Mark these three locations in your Bible for future reference, because they are primary. Several secondary chapters also provide other important details; these include mainly 1 Peter 4, 1 Corinthians 7, 1 Corinthians 13–14 and Ephesians 3.

I will begin putting our master list of gifts together by using the three primary chapters. The words in parentheses are variant translations found in several English versions of the Bible.

Romans 12:6-8 mentions the following spiritual gifts:

1. Prophecy (preaching, inspired utterance)
2. Service (ministry)
3. Teaching
4. Exhortation (stimulating faith, encouraging)
5. Giving (contributing, generosity, sharing)
6. Leadership (authority, ruling, administration)
7. Mercy (sympathy, comfort to the sorrowing, showing kindness)

First Corinthians 12:8-10,28 adds (without repeating those already listed from Romans):

8. Wisdom (wise advice, wise speech)
9. Knowledge (studying, speaking with knowledge)
10. Faith
11. Healing
12. Miracles (doing great deeds)
13. Discerning of spirits (discrimination in spiritual matters)
14. Tongues (speaking in languages never learned, ecstatic utterance)
15. Interpretation of tongues
16. Apostle
17. Helps
18. Administration (governments, getting others to work together)

Ephesians 4:11 adds (again, without repeating any of the above):

19. Evangelist
20. Pastor (caring for God's people)

COMPLETING THE MASTER LIST

The three primary chapters give us 20 separate gifts, but that is not all that there are.

One thing becomes immediately evident from looking at these three primary lists—none of the lists is complete in itself. Some gifts mentioned in Ephesians are mentioned in Romans, and some in Romans are mentioned in 1 Corinthians, and some in 1 Corinthians are mentioned in Ephesians. Apparently, none of them is intended to be a complete catalog of the gifts God gives. And we could surmise that if none of the three lists is complete in itself, probably the three lists together, or the 20 gifts, are not complete.

The Bible itself confirms that this is a correct assumption. At least five other gifts are mentioned in the New Testament:

21. Celibacy, or continence (see 1 Cor. 7:7)
22. Voluntary poverty (see 1 Cor. 13:3)
23. Martyrdom (see 1 Cor. 13:3)
24. Missionary (see Eph. 3:6-8)
25. Hospitality (see 1 Pet. 4:9)

DETERMINING WHETHER ALL GIFTS ARE MENTIONED IN THE BIBLE

These 25 spiritual gifts are all those mentioned in the Bible as gifts. But this biblical list, as I have said, is apparently not intended to be exhaustive. Now this raises an interesting question. Could it be that there are some legitimate spiritual gifts that God gives to certain believers which are not mentioned specifically as gifts in the Bible? Naturally there are two possible answers to this question, and each of the answers has its supporting points. So if you feel that it is best to leave the list with 25, I would not quarrel with you. But my own personal conclusion is that some other real gifts are actually in use.

I have come to this conclusion after years of observation. I think that there are at least two, possibly three, spiritual gifts that are not referred to as such in Scripture. The ministries that they are designed to accomplish are definitely biblical. But don't ask me for verses that call them spiritual gifts per se.

I was gratified when I read the works of several other scholars who agree. A number of them mention three gifts, which they suggest adding but which I have chosen *not* to add, namely: craftsmanship, preaching and writing. I must admit that I do not have really strong arguments against adding these, so I leave the question open.

But in the material on spiritual gifts that I have produced up to now, I have added two others, because my empirical observation of Church life and ministry has lead me to the inescapable conclusion that, yes, there are spiritual gifts of intercession and deliverance. That would bring my total from 25 up to 27.

However, as readers of many of my other books would know, I have more recently transitioned from traditional Christianity to the New Apostolic Reformation. One of the big differences, among many others, is that worship in apostolic churches is radically different from worship in traditional churches. I have now observed something which was not on my radar screen when I did my previous books on spiritual gifts, and that is that there is a spiritual gift of leading worship. It is more than musical skills. It is a God-given ability to usher others into the very presence of

God in an extraordinary way. I think I made a mistake in limiting my previous lists to 27 gifts; there should be 28:

26. Intercession
27. Deliverance (exorcism, casting out demons)
28. Leading worship (music)

This is what I mean when I say I prefer an open-ended approach to the spiritual gifts. I like to see flexibility in things like this. I had many second thoughts about excluding leading worship from my original list of 27 gifts, and because I take an open-ended view, I now have no problem adding it and making the list 28 gifts. I must apologize, however, for the fact that at this point I cannot add this gift to the Wagner-Modified Houts Questionnaire.

Distinguishing Gifts from Offices

Some may observe the fact that the list of spiritual gifts in Ephesians 4 is slightly different from the other two because it mentions *offices* rather than *gifts* as such. This is correct. When it speaks of apostles, prophets, evangelists, pastors and teachers, which I like to call the foundational, or governmental, offices, being given to the Church (see Eph. 4:11), the focus is thereby placed on gifted people who have also been recognized in such official positions. Usually such people have been ordained, or commissioned, with a public laying on of hands.

You can have a gift without an office, but you cannot have an office without a gift. You can have the gift of prophecy without being recognized as a prophet. The office is the official recognition on the part of the Body of Christ that a person has a certain spiritual gift, or a gift-mix, and that such a person is authorized to use that gift in public ministry. We are most accustomed to doing that with the gift of pastor and recognizing it through what we call ordination. Ordination does not give a person the gift of pastor—it assumes that God has already done that. Rather, ordination is an affirmation that responsible people have observed that the candidate has the gift and that it should be recognized by the rest of the Body.

RECOGNIZING THAT EVERY GIFT IS IN THE MINORITY

Since obviously not everyone is a pastor or a prophet or an apostle, this raises an important general principle relating to spiritual gifts: More members of the Body of Christ *do not* share any particular spiritual gift than those who *do* share it. Just about everyone would agree, for example, that more Christians do not have the gift of celibacy than have it. This applies to every gift on the list, whether evangelist or teaching or hospitality or service or discerning of spirits or whatever.

This is reinforced by the biblical analogy of the physical body as the model through which we are to understand spiritual gifts. We know that in our own human bodies the majority of members are not hands. More members are not eyes, kidneys, chins, tongues or elbows than are. God has determined that we have two eyes, and this is just enough to do the job of seeing on behalf of the hundreds of other members of the same body. A tongue, for example, does not need to see. The Bible says specifically that the whole body should not be an eye, because if it were, it could not hear or smell (see 1 Cor. 12:17).

I believe that it is reasonable to conclude that probably less than 50 percent of the Body should ordinarily be expected to have any particular gift. My hunch is that most of the percentages will come out far less than 50 percent. I have done some research on the gift of evangelist, for example, and found that the figure is probably around 5 percent. The gift of missionary is less than 1 percent and the gift of intercession around 5 percent. Just like we don't need three eyes, we don't need more of gifts like these. God assigns the gifts and also determines the ratio of the gifts.

PAIRING UP: HYPHENATED GIFTS

Some make a point that in Ephesians 4:11 the gifts most often listed as "pastor" and "teacher" should not be separate, but they should be combined as "pastor-teacher." They argue that it is a kind of dual gift, not two different gifts.

In my opinion, however, there is a better way to explain such things. I think that many of the gifts very frequently pair up with each other and that it most helpful to regard them as hyphenated gifts. For example, not every teacher is a pastor and not every pastor is a teacher. But a large number of people are pastor-teachers because they have been given both gifts.

There are several other natural pairings of gifts. I think, for example, of intercession-prophecy or knowledge-teaching or deliverance-discerning of spirits or apostle-leadership or healing-miracles, to name a few.

HONORING ALL VARIATIONS AND DEGREES OF GIFTS

Within almost every one of the 28 spiritual gifts will be found a wide range of variations and degrees. The cue for this might be seen in 1 Corinthians 12:4-6 where it speaks of gifts *(charismaton)*, ministries *(diakonion)* and activities *(energematon)*. Ray Stedman defines ministry as "the sphere in which a gift is performed," and an activity (or working) as "the degree of power by which a gift is manifested or ministered on a specific occasion."[1]

A person who has the gift of evangelist, for example, might be a personal evangelist or a public evangelist—different ministries within the same gift. One public evangelist might be an international celebrity who fills stadiums with 50,000 people and sees 3,000 conversions in a week. Another public evangelist might minister mostly in churches that hold 500 people and see 30 conversions in a week. In the final analysis, both may be found to be equally faithful in the exercise of their gift.

Variations and degrees, as the gifts themselves, are distributed at the discretion of God. Just as the master in the parable of the talents gave to one five talents, to another two and to yet another one, so God in His wisdom gives to each of us "a measure of faith" (Rom. 12:3). This is why, when gifts are in operation properly, Christians who have different degrees of the same gift have no cause for jealousy or envy. My left hand is not envious of my right hand because it may not be able to develop skills equal to my right hand. Rather, the two hands work together harmoniously for the benefit of the whole body. God has given me a gift for writing, for example, but in a relatively moderate degree. I am realistic enough to know that scores of others—Martin Marty and George Otis, Jr., and John Stott, to name a few—have such a high degree of the gift that I am not worthy to be mentioned in the same breath.

CLASSIFYING THE GIFTS

The gifts can be classified in many different ways. Bill Gothard, for example, divides them into "motivations," "ministries" and "manifestations."[2] Some Reformed theologians have separated "ordinary gifts" from "extraordinary gifts." I have seen gifts divided into "enabling gifts," "servicing gifts" and "tongues/interpretation." There could be others.

Some of the people who use these classifications have had excellent success in teaching Christians to discover, develop and use their spiritual gifts. I applaud whatever classification they use as long as it works. Obviously, none of these humanly designed classifications is divinely inspired.

In my own teaching, as I have said before, I prefer the open-ended approach. I do not find it particularly helpful to classify the gifts. The reason I have taken this route is not necessarily because I think it may be any more biblical than the others but simply because I have found it to be the most helpful approach for my own particular teaching style. It works well for me, and it may work for you as well.

Notes

1. Ray C. Stedman, *Body Life* (Ventura, CA: Regal Books, 1972), pp. 40-41.
2. Bill Gothard, source unknown.

Four Danger Signs TO AVOID

I'm not an alarmist by nature, but I fear that the Body of Christ, at least in the United States, is in great danger of getting off track in the vital area of spiritual gifts. George Barna, lauded by many as the foremost researcher of the Christian Church today, has released some startling information. When I read it, it was a wake-up call for me. I confess that during the decade of the 1990s, I had put teaching spiritual gifts on the back burner. But I no longer can do this. God used Barna's research to speak to me clearly about teaching this subject much more. In fact, this book is one of the immediate outcomes.

BARNA'S FINDINGS

First, and most disturbing, George Barna found that a remarkable number of born-again Christians who have heard of spiritual gifts do not think that they have any spiritual gifts at all. And unfortunately, this number is growing.

Here are the facts: In 1995 the percentage of born-again adults who did not think that they had a spiritual gift was 4 percent. Not too alarming. But by 2000 that number had risen to 21 percent! Very alarming! If this trend continues, we will soon have a dangerously sick Body on our hands!

Second, Barna found that too many Christians had bizarre ideas of what spiritual gifts really were. They thought that some of the gifts were a sense of humor, going to church, a good personality, poetry, survival, friendliness and other things that were far from what the Bible teaches.[1]

THE STATE OF THE CHURCH

George Barna's responsibility is to get the facts. Others of us are responsible for interpreting these facts and discovering what is going on. As I worked on processing this data, I came to some conclusions. I may not see the full picture, but I believe that it is important for me to share my thoughts, even though they might be a bit unpopular in certain circles.

Between 1995 and 2000, the churches of what I call the New Apostolic Reformation became the fastest-growing group of churches in the United States.[2] While these churches have tremendous strengths, unfortunately, with some exceptions, their teaching and practice of mobilizing their church members to do the work of the ministry through spiritual gifts are surprisingly weak. If this observation is correct, it would explain, at least to a considerable extent, Barna's conclusions.

Where does this weakness come from? The genealogy of the New Apostolic Reformation goes back to the independent charismatic movement. The genealogy of the independent charismatic movement goes back to classical Pentecostalism. We are thankful for the role that classical Pentecostalism has played in surfacing the true biblical view of the person and work of the Holy Spirit, the third Person of the Trinity. The kingdom of God would never be where it is today if it weren't for the Pentecostal pioneers in the early part of the last century.

However, while Pentecostals helped us become aware that spiritual gifts were for today, they incorporated two serious errors con-

cerning spiritual gifts in their teachings. These errors were perpetuated by many independent charismatic leaders and they have also
carried over to many New Apostolic Reformation leaders. If we do
not correct these two errors, at least in my opinion, the Church will
soon be on a downhill slide.

What are these two serious errors?

The Short List of Spiritual Gifts

Classical Pentecostalism teaches that there are nine gifts of the
Holy Spirit, all found in the first part of 1 Corinthians 12. They
would include wisdom, knowledge, faith, healing, miracles,
prophecy, discerning of spirits, tongues and interpretation of
tongues. Pentecostal leaders encourage believers to use spiritual
gifts, but their teaching and writing on spiritual gifts deal only
with this short list, not the 28 that I listed in the last chapter or
any other longer list.

While these nine gifts are essential for the saints to do the
work of the ministry, there are many other functions of the Body
of Christ that are also necessary for it to function as God
designed it. Believers who think that there are only nine gifts
and who do not happen to minister regularly in any of them will
likely be among Barna's 21 percent who think they have no gift
at all. They may have one or more of the other 19 gifts, but they
have not been taught to recognize them as legitimate gifts.

The "Situational View" of Spiritual Gifts

Classical Pentecostalism has taught that all of the spiritual gifts
(all nine, that is) are available to all believers depending on the
situation. If the situation arises when a gift such as prophecy or
healing or wisdom or whatever would be useful, God will give
such a gift to any believer. But when that situation passes, they
might not have the gift ever again or they might get it only occasionally. This is known as the "situational view."

A quick review of the last couple of chapters will show that the situational view is not biblical. The biblical teaching is that our spiritual gifts are like members of our human body. Members of the body such as ears or necks or stomachs or vocal chords are not ears or necks or stomachs or vocal chords for a one-time use or to be used occasionally. They are constitutionally parts of the body as long as the body is healthy. The view that I am teaching in this book is the *constitutional* view of spiritual gifts as opposed to the *situational* view.

I think I can explain quite briefly how this erroneous teaching crept into classical Pentecostalism. Once Pentecostals started believing in and teaching the baptism in the Holy Spirit, many believers began speaking in tongues. History shows the early Pentecostal leaders were typically not among those who liked to spend much time in biblical exegesis or theologizing. They knew that tongues was called a spiritual gift, so they assumed that everyone who spoke in tongues must have the gift of tongues. Some Pentecostal believers, in fact, ended up speaking in tongues only once in their lives. So the conclusion was that they had received the gift of tongues for only that one situation. This situational view was subsequently applied to the other eight gifts on the list as well. When later generations produced Pentecostal biblical scholars, they searched and found arguments to justify the position of their predecessors.

The situational view of spiritual gifts could easily have been avoided if Pentecostal leaders had understood the important distinction between spiritual gifts and Christian roles. I will detail this in the next chapter as a better way to explain why some believers speak in tongues all the time (the gift) and others perhaps only once (the role).

The situational approach to spiritual gifts, especially when applied to only nine of the gifts, will inevitably weaken the Church internally. I remember hearing from a new apostolic leader a sermon entitled "How to Flow in the Nine Gifts of the Holy Spirit." This sermon combined the two errors of classical Pentecostalism that have been perpetuated in the New Apostolic Reformation today. Fortunately, George Barna has brought to the public eye some of the disturbing effects of this teaching—in time for it to be corrected, I hope.

SPIRITUAL GIFTS: LIFETIME POSSESSIONS

This raises the question of how long we keep a spiritual gift once God gives it to us.

In my opinion, once a person is given a bona fide spiritual gift, it is a lifetime possession. I derive this from Romans 12:4, where, once again, Paul gives us the analogy of the physical body as the hermeneutical key for understanding spiritual gifts. If spiritual gifts are to the Body of Christ as spinal columns or skin or other members are to the physical body, there is little question in my mind that once we know what our gift is, we can depend on keeping it. I do not go to bed at night having any worry whatsoever that tomorrow my hand might wake up a kidney. Both the development of the spiritual gifts in the life of an individual Christian and the smooth operation of the Body of Christ as a whole depend on similar confidence.

However, this does not mean that the gifts we have today will be the sum total of the gifts we have the rest of our lives. God gives us our initial gifts when we are born again. But later in life we might discover that we have and are using gifts that we never used before. There are two ways to explain this. Either we always had the gift and it just surfaced, or God decided to give us a new gift. I think that both of these things are likely to happen. For example, I know that I now have the gifts of healing, giving and apostle, but 20 years ago I had no awareness of having these gifts.

The point is that we should always be open to moving in new areas of ministry as God determines. We should never be stuck in the mud, so to speak.

DOMINANT AND SUBORDINATE GIFTS

Multigifted people may find that at certain periods of their ministry some of their gifts will be dominant and others subordinate. This ranking order might vary over the years as circumstances change. In my opinion, however, this does not mean that a gift has been lost along the way. I know that I have the gift of missionary, for instance, but it has been relatively dormant for some years now.

At the same time, there is a danger that some gifts may become dormant against God's will. You may have a gift that you are supposed to be using but are not. This seemed to be what Paul had in mind when he had to keep exhorting Timothy: "Do not neglect the gift" (1 Tim. 4:14) and "stir up the gift" (2 Tim. 1:6) and "do the work of an evangelist" (2 Tim. 4:5), on the obvious assumption that one of Timothy's spiritual gifts was the gift of evangelist. Allowing gifts to become dormant is one of the ways we are in danger of "quench[ing] the Spirit" (1 Thess. 5:19), and we need to avoid that at all costs.

ABUSE OF SPIRITUAL GIFTS

We need to face the unfortunate fact that spiritual gifts can be abused in many ways. In a short book like this, I will not attempt to catalog and comment on all the abuses of spiritual gifts common today. But I do want to name and comment on the two that I consider to be especially widespread and counterproductive in the Church.

Gift Exaltation

The first abuse is *gift exaltation*. In some circles, it is popular to exalt one gift over the others. Having a certain gift seems to constitute a spiritual status symbol in some groups. First-class citizens tend to be separated from second-class citizens on the basis of exercising a certain gift or combination of gifts.

When this happens, gifts can easily become ends in themselves. They can glorify the user rather than the giver. They can benefit the individual more than than the Body. They can produce pride and self-indulgence. The Corinthians had fallen into this trap, exalting the gift of tongues, and Paul writes 1 Corinthians 12—14 in an attempt to straighten them out. All of us need to take fair warning and avoid gift exaltation.

The Syndrome of Gift Projection

The second abuse is *gift projection*. Most Christians who have biographies written about themselves have accomplished extraordinary things during their lifetimes. What gave them the ability to turn in the kind of lifetime performance that would justify a biography? It has to be that God had given them a spiritual gift or gifts in an unusual degree, that they developed them conscientiously and that they used them to the glory of God and for the benefit of the Body of Christ.

Few biographers, however, and few heroes of their biographies have been people who are sensitive to the biblical teaching on spiritual gifts. This has caused them to take another approach toward explaining the cause of their unusual feats. What frequently happens is that readers are led to believe that so-and-so accomplished extraordinary things simply because that person loved God so much. Ergo, if you loved God that much, dear reader, you could do the same thing. If you are not able to do these things, you now know the reason why. Something is deficient in your relationship with God.

However, many Christians who read these biographies are, in fact, totally consecrated to God. Because of this, they are often the ones who feel the most frustrated, guilty and defeated when they learn about these giants of the faith. To make matters worse, when the heroes of the biographies are ignorant of spiritual gifts, they sometimes engage in what I call gift projection. They seem to say "Look, I'm just an ordinary Christian, no different from anyone else. Here's what I do, and God blesses it. Consequently, if you just do what I do, God will bless you in the same way." What they rarely say, unfortunately, is "I can do what I do because God has given me a certain gift or gift-mix. If you discover that God has given you the same, join me in this. If not, I don't expect you to be like me. You do what God has equipped you to do, and we will love and help each other as different members of the Body."

People caught up in the syndrome of gift projection seem to want the whole body to be an eye. They unwittingly impose guilt and shame on fellow Christians who are not like them. They make feet say, "Because I am not a hand, I am not of the body," (1 Cor. 12:15). They usually have little idea how devastating gift projection can be for those who have different gifts. They would be like the steward in the parable who came back with ten talents saying to the one who came back with four, "If you only loved the master more, you would have come back with ten also," without mentioning that the master gave him five talents to start with but gave the other only two.

Today, more than ever before, we need a healthy, biblical view of spiritual gifts. Let's begin by avoiding the common errors and moving strongly ahead according to God's design for the Body of Christ.

Notes

1. See "Awareness of Spiritual Gifts Is Changing," News Release from Barna Research Group, Ltd., (Ventura, CA), February 5, 2001, pp. 1-2.
2. For details on the New Apostolic Reformation, see my books *The New Apostolic Churches* (Ventura, CA: Regal Books, 1998) and *Churchquake!* (Ventura, CA: Regal Books, 1999).

CHAPTER 5

Clearing Away
THE CONFUSION

As we go about discovering, developing and using our spiritual gifts, it is important to keep a clear head. Experience has shown that there are four areas of confusion that frequently arise in the process. They relate to natural talents, the fruit of the Spirit, Christian roles and counterfeit gifts. Let's look at them one at a time.

DON'T CONFUSE SPIRITUAL GIFTS WITH NATURAL TALENTS

Every human being, by virtue of being made in the image of God, possesses certain natural talents. As with spiritual gifts, the natural talents have different variations and degrees. Talents are one of the features that give every human being a unique personality. Part of our self-identity is wrapped up in the particular mix of talents we have.

Where do these natural talents come from? Ultimately, of course, they are given by God. Consequently, in the broadest sense of the word they should be recognized as God-given gifts. That is why we often say of a person who sings well or who has an extraordinary IQ or who can hit a golf ball into a hole from a long distance, "My, isn't that person gifted?" By this, however, we should not imply that they have *spiritual* gifts.

Having natural talents has nothing directly to do with being a Christian or being a member of the Body of Christ. Many Muslims, Hindus and atheists, for example, have superb talents for art, medicine, literature and other things. They have natural talents, but they do not have spiritual gifts. And the ultimate source of these talents, of course, is God the Creator.

Years ago when I was living in the Los Angeles area the Los Angeles Lakers were dominating the world of professional basketball. One of their players, Kareem Abdul Jabbar, had an incredible talent for throwing the basketball into the hoop. No one has ever scored more points in a lifetime than he did. Another one of the players, A. C. Green, had a similar talent. Kareem Abdul Jabbar was a committed Muslim. A. C. Green was a committed, witnessing Christian, a member of the Body of Christ. Their choice of whom to worship had nothing to do with those natural talents. In fact, day in and day out, the Muslim scored more than the Christian.

While Christians, like anyone else, have natural talents, these talents should not be confused with spiritual gifts. It is technically incorrect and unbiblical for Christians to say that their gift is fixing automobiles, gourmet cooking, telling jokes, painting pictures or playing basketball.

To make matters worse, the Greek biblical word *charisma* has been secularized. I understand that in Greek literature the apostle Paul is the only known author who uses "charisma" frequently. The only other recorded appearances of "charisma" in Greek literature, if I understand it correctly, are in 1 Peter 4:10 and once in Philo's writings. But a century ago a famous German sociologist, Max Weber, began to use the word "charisma" to describe a certain kind of dynamic leader, whom he called a "charismatic leader." His word "charismatic" had no theological overtones. In Weber's sense, the word has continued to be used in secular circles. Sociologists would regard an Adolf Hitler or a Joseph Stalin or a Dali Lama as having "charisma" in the broad sense of the word. But none of the three, as far as I know, would have considered himself a member of the Body of Christ, and thus none of them has been given a spiritual gift.

Spiritual gifts are reserved exclusively for Christians. No unbeliever has one, and every true believer in Jesus does. Spiritual gifts are not to be regarded as dedicated natural talents. The two may have a discernible relationship, however, because in many cases (not all, by any means) God may take an unbeliever's natural talent and transform it into a spiritual gift when that person is saved and becomes a member of the Body of Christ. But in such a case the spiritual gift is more than just a souped-up natural talent. Because it is given by God, a spiritual gift can never be cloned.

Consider, for example, the natural talent of teaching. A significant segment of the population are teachers by profession. But as most every pastor knows, not every well-trained, competent public-school teacher turns out to be be a good Sunday School teacher. Why? In those cases, God evidently did not choose to transform the *talent* of teaching into the *gift* of teaching. But in many other cases He does that very thing, and the schoolteachers become excellent Sunday School teachers.

While God frequently transforms a natural talent into a spiritual gift, at the same time many spiritual gifts have nothing to do with a person's natural talent. I mentioned a while back that I have a gift of healing. Nothing in my background as an unbeliever would have hinted that this would happen. As I write this, one of the most famous public speakers in the country is Benny Hinn. When Benny was an unbeliever, he had a serious speech impediment! His eloquence as a preacher was a completely new thing that God did for him after he was saved.

Don't Confuse Spiritual Gifts with the Fruit of the Spirit

The fruit of the Spirit is described in Galatians 5:22-23: "love, joy, peace, longsuffering, kindness, goodness, faithfulness, gentleness, self-control." Some Bible expositors point out that "fruit" is in the singular and that the original Greek construction would permit a colon after "love." So although all these other things are part of the fruit of the Spirit, love could well be the primary one.

Notice that in the list of 28 spiritual gifts in the last chapter, none of them is love. Love is not a spiritual gift. It is improper to speak of the gift of love, if by "gift" we mean that love should be seen as spiritual gift number 29 on our list. In the broad sense, of course, love is a gift from God and should be so regarded. "We love [God] because He first loved us" (1 John 4:19). But love is not a charisma in the sense that God gives it to some members of the Body but not to others.

The fruit of the Spirit is the normal, expected outcome of Christian growth, maturity, holiness, Christlikeness and fullness of the Holy Spirit. Because all Christians have the responsibility of growing in their faith, all have the responsibility of developing the fruit of the Spirit. Fruit are not *discovered* as are the gifts, they are *developed* through the believer's walk with God and through yielding to the Holy Spirit. Although spiritual gifts help define what a Christian *does*, the fruit of the Spirit help define what a Christian *is*.

The fruit of the Spirit is the indispensable foundation for the effective exercise of spiritual gifts. Gifts without fruit may really be gifts, but they are worthless. The Corinthian believers found this out the hard way. They had an ideal gift-mix, according to 1 Corinthians 1:7. They were busy discovering, developing and using their spiritual gifts. They were as charismatic as a church can get. Yet they were a spiritual disaster area, one of the most messed-up churches we read about in the New Testament.

How can you be a church filled with born-again believers, excited about all the spiritual gifts, and still be impotent in the sight of God? You can, if you don't have the fruit of the Spirit along with the gifts.

The basic problem of the Corinthians, therefore, was not gifts but the fruit. That is why Paul wrote 1 Corinthians 13 to them. In it, he waxed eloquently about love, one of the fruit of the Spirit. He told them they could have the gift of tongues, the gift of prophecy, the gift of knowledge, the gift of faith, the gift of voluntary poverty, the gift of martyrdom and any other gift, but without love the gifts amounted to absolutely nothing (see 1 Cor. 13:1-3). Gifts without fruit are like an automobile tire without air—the ingredients may be all together, but they are worthless and they will not do what they are intended to do.

Keep in mind also that gifts are temporal, but fruit is eternal. In 1 Corinthians 13 we are also told that gifts such as prophecy, tongues and knowledge will vanish away, but faith, hope and love will abide. Whereas gifts are task oriented, fruit are God-oriented.

It is worth noting that a passage on fruit accompanies every one of the four primary passages on gifts. First Corinthians 13 is the most explicit and most widely recognized, following 1 Corinthians 12 where the gifts are featured. But also, the list of gifts ending in Romans 12:8 is immediately followed by "let love be without hypocrisy" and "be kindly affectionate to one another with brotherly love" (vv. 9-10). The passage on fruit continues for another 11 verses. Then in Ephesians 4, the gift passage ends with verse 16 and the fruit passage picks up in the next verse and carries through the next chapter. Among other things it says, "Walk in love, as Christ also has loved us" (Eph. 5:2). The passage on spiritual gifts beginning with 1 Peter 4:9 is immediately preceded with "above all things have fervent love for one another, for 'love will cover a multitude of sins'" (v. 8).

DON'T CONFUSE SPIRITUAL GIFTS WITH CHRISTIAN ROLES

When we look at the list of 28 gifts, it becomes obvious that many of them describe activities expected of every Christian, whether they have gifts or not. At this point, it is necessary to distinguish between *spiritual gifts* and *Christian roles*. Roles are slightly different from the fruit of the Spirit in that they involve more doing than being. But they are similar to the fruit in that they are characteristic of every concientious Christian.

You have a spiritual gift, as I have previously explained in detail, because God has chosen to give you that gift once you become a member of the Body of Christ. You have certain Christian roles simply because you are born again, and your new nature causes you to do certain things that are also expected of every other believer. Let's look at several examples.

Perhaps the most obvious spiritual gift that relates directly to a Christian role is faith. Just becoming a Christian and first entering into the Body of Christ requires faith. No one can be a Christian without faith. And this faith, according to the Bible, is a gift of God (see Eph. 2:8-9). Then we are later told that faithfulness is a part of the fruit of the Spirit (see Gal. 5:22) and that "without faith it is impossible to please [God]" (Heb. 11:6). In other words, the lifestyle of every Christian, without exception, is to be characterized by day-in, day-out faith. This is our "role" of faith.

Over and above this, however, the spiritual "gift" of faith is given by God to relatively few members of the Body. This *gift* of faith is much more than the *fruit* of faith or the *role* of faith, both of which we expect to see in every true Christian. I love to be around those with the gift of faith, even though I have never suspected that I was personally gifted in that area.

The gift of hospitality provides another example of this difference. Neither my wife, Doris, nor I have that particular gift. We are happiest in our home when no one else is around. Our personality tests show that neither one of us is sanguine. However, we do have a *role* of entertaining guests in our home, and we do it with some regularity. Having people over for dinner, occasionally putting up a person for the night, taking a visitor on an outing, hosting parties, loaning our car and making sure that new people are oriented to the community are all included in our Christian roles. None of these things comes easily to us, and we are aware that we do not do it as often or as well as we should. But we do make a conscientious effort because doing it is simply part of living the life of a good Christian.

I believe that another role of every Christian believer is to tithe their income to God's work. I am appalled when I read statistics that show that American church members average under 3 percent of their income in giving. Ten percent, biblically speaking, is only a starting point because that amount does not belong to us, it belongs to God. Using it for ourselves amounts to robbing God and it brings a curse (see Mal. 3:8-9). True giving only starts with our offerings from the 90 percent which God has given to us. What I'm saying here is that tithing is not a spiritual gift, nor is giving offerings above that—these are Christian roles. Still, some believers have the gift of giving and the percentage they give is far higher than what God expects of those who do not have the gift.

Prayer is another example of a Christian role: Prayer is the privilege and responsibility of every Christian. No spiritual gift is needed for a vital prayer life. One does not need the gift of intercession to talk to God, but some have a gift of intercession and they have a prayer-relationship with God that far exceeds what most of us experience on a regular basis. Spending two, three or five hours in prayer every day is part of an intercessor's lifestyle.

Let me mention a few others: Some have the spiritual gift of service, but nevertheless all Christians should serve one another (see Gal. 5:13). Some have the spiritual gift of exhortation, but all believers have a general role of exhorting one another (see Heb. 10:25). A few have the gift of evangelist, but all Christians are expected to exercise their role of witness (see Acts 1:8).

Let's go back to George Barna's research. I suggested when I brought it up that one of the reasons why ignorance of spiritual gifts is on the increase in the American church may be the influence of the *situational* over the *constitutional* view of spiritual gifts. I also suggested that one way to avoid the unbiblical situational view is to understand the difference between spiritual gifts and Christian roles. Now let me explain.

I know one pastor who wanted power healing to be a prominent feature of the life and ministry of his church. He did not want to be seen as a superstar faith healer, but rather he wanted to equip all the believers in his church to lay hands on the sick, pray for them and see them healed. This is the good news. The bad news is that he erroneously thought that in order to do this, all the believers needed the spiritual gift of healing. So he switched from the constitutional view of spiritual gifts, which he had previously been teaching, to the situational view. The healing ministry of the church had a good surge, but it subsequently could not be sustained.

It would have been much better to have taught the people that every one of them had a Christian role of laying hands on the sick and praying for their healing, just like they had a role of giving tithes and offerings, of interceding for others or of being a good witness to unbelievers. None of these things requires a gift. Nevertheless, God does give spiritual gifts of healing, giving, intercession and evangelist to certain members of the Body whom He chooses. This is the biblical formula for a healthy Church.

If believers think that they will be given any and all of the gifts according to the situation they find themselves in, their minds become closed to the possibility that God will give them one or more gifts that they have to be responsible to develop and use on a consistent basis. They will easily fall into the 21 percent reflected in Barna's research who do not think that they have any real spiritual gift at all. This erroneous belief weakens the whole Body of Christ.

DON'T CONFUSE SPIRITUAL GIFTS WITH COUNTERFEIT GIFTS

I wish I did not have to write this section on counterfeit gifts. I wish it were not true that Satan and his demons and evil spirits are real and actively opposing the work of the Lord. Jesus Himself said, "For false christs and false prophets will rise and show great signs and wonders to deceive, if possible, even the elect" (Matt. 24:24). Jesus also speaks about those who prophesy and cast out demons in His name but who, in reality, turn out to be workers of iniquity (see Matt. 7:22-23).

I do not doubt that Satan can and does counterfeit every gift on the list. He is a supernatural being and he has supernatural powers. His power was shown in a spectacular way in Egypt when Pharaoh's magicians could publicly match some of the supernatural works that God did through Moses (see Exod. 7—8). Of course, Satan's power is limited and controlled. In Egypt he could match God's works only to a certain extent.

A rather chilling book on this subject, entitled *The Challenging Counterfeit*, was written by Raphael Gasson, now a Christian but formerly a spiritualist medium. He tells it like it is. Gasson's experience has shown him that "It is very obvious that Satan is using an extremely subtle counterfeit to the precious gifts of the Spirit."[1] In his book, Gasson describes in detail several of Satan's favorite counterfeits.

Gasson specifically shows, for example, how false gifts of faith, miracles, healing, tongues and interpretation are produced by Satan. The counterfeit of the gift of discerning spirits, he feels, is clairvoyance and clairaudience. The gift of deliverance is cleverly reproduced by the devil as well, and this is one of the reasons I do not like to refer to it as the gift of exorcism.

Gasson recalls how Satan gave him the ability to prophesy, as he does many other fortune-tellers, and points out that most of these counterfeit prophecies came true. This is one way the devil makes his appeals more attractive. Psychics can earn a living by receiving information from the invisible world through agents of the devil.

On one occasion during the World War II years, for example, a man brought to Gasson an item belonging to the man's son who was in the military. The man wanted to find out where his son was. Through his "spirit guide," who purported to be the spirit of an African witch doctor, Gasson found out that the owner of the item was well and a prisoner of war. The father then proceeded to show Gasson a telegram from the War Department stating that his son had been killed in action more than two weeks previously. Gasson went back to his guide and verified that the soldier-son really was not dead and that the father would have this confirmed in three days. Sure enough, three days later the father received a telegram from the War Department apologizing for the mistake and saying that the boy was well and a prisoner of war.

Some mistakenly interpret this kind of prophecy as a work of God. It is in reality the clever counterfeit of the devil. But it is no less real.

We immediately need to remind ourselves that God knows all about this deceitfulness and that He has given adequate power to

His children to prevent it. One of my colleagues on the Lausanne Committee for World Evangelization was Petrus Octavianus of Indonesia. On one occasion, he was speaking to an audience of 3,000 people in Stuttgart, Germany. At the end of his presentation, he asked for a time of silent prayer. When all was quiet, one man on the platform got up and began praying in tongues. Petrus Octavianus turned to him and in the name of Jesus commanded him to be silent. Octavianus later explained, "After I had prayed for clarity, it became clear to me that this speaking in tongues was not brought about by the Holy Spirit but by the enemy." It turned out to be true and the man was exposed as a fraud.

It is essential to keep in mind that "He who is in you is greater than he who is in the world" (1 John 4:4). Knowing that Satan is active should not end up making us timid. We receive spiritual gifts from God Himself as He fills us with the Holy Spirit. He will overrule all the efforts of the enemy to confuse us about our true, bona fide spiritual gifts. God is determined that you, and every other true member of the Body of Christ, will fulfill the destiny that He has for you through fruitful ministry with your spiritual gifts.

Note

1. Raphael Gasson, *The Challenging Counterfeit* (Plainfield, New Jersey: Logos International, 1979), p. 90.

CHAPTER 6

THE FIVE STEPS FOR
Discovering Your
SPIRITUAL GIFTS

Nowhere does the Bible deal specifically with finding gifts. Nowhere does Peter or Paul or James say, "And now, brethren, I would have you follow these steps to discover your spiritual gifts." The lack of such a passage has convinced some that discovering gifts is an improper pursuit for Christians. I disagree.

In my opinion, the lack of such specific instructions in the Bible should not be a deterrent to set forth practical, twenty-first-century procedures for knowing and doing God's will. Nowhere does the Bible tells us how to draw up the constitution and bylaws for a local church or what church membership requirements should be. Nowhere does the Bible tell us how to organize a missionary sending agency or how to support missionaries. For centuries, theologians and Bible students have been trying to determine exactly when and how Christians should be baptized. Most Christians do not regard this as a stumbling block.

On this particular issue of spiritual gifts, I am not alone. Most authors of current books on spiritual gifts include information on how to discover your gift. Most of them, in fact, are saying just about the same thing. Authors try not to copy each other, so each one develops a different way of saying it. But the procedure for finding gifts is surprisingly similar from author to author. This is comforting, because it does seem that a consensus has been emerging, which helps reduce confusion and increase effectiveness throughout the Church. In any case, we who are in the field of teaching spiritual gifts are much closer to agreement with each other on how to do it than those, for example, who are dealing with issues of baptism or events surrounding the second coming of Christ.

BE MINDFUL OF THE FOUR FUNDAMENTAL PREREQUISITES

Before beginning to take the actual steps toward finding your gift, four fundamental prerequisites need to characterize your life. Leave out any one of them, and you will have a very difficult time discovering your gift.

First, you have to be a Christian. Spiritual gifts are given only to members of the Body of Christ. Unfortunately, not all church members in America are truly members of the Body of Christ. Almost all churches, some more than others, have members who are not personally committed to Jesus. They may attend with some regularity, put money in the offering plate and even belong to some boards or committees and teach Sunday School. But they have never come into that personal relationship with the Savior that some call being born again or others call commitment to Christ or being saved or converted. The term used is much less important than the idea it conveys, namely, an actual personal relationship with Jesus Christ.

Second, you have to believe in spiritual gifts. I am almost certain that the reason that some born-again Christians do not believe in spiritual gifts is simply that no one has told them about spiritual gifts. In my experience, I cannot recall any Christian who has seriously listened to teaching on spiritual gifts and not recognized that these gifts are for today—and for them.

This becomes a question of faith. You must believe that God has given you a spiritual gift before you start the process of discovering it. Earlier I tried to make the best case possible to prove that every Christian, including you, has one or more spiritual gifts. If you haven't been convinced, the five steps in this chapter may not be for you. For the steps to work, you must have a sense of gratitude to God that He has given you a gift, and a sense of joyful anticipation in finding out what it is.

Third, you have to be willing to work. The five steps I am about to suggest constitute a spiritual exercise, and God's help is needed to accomplish it. God has given you one or more spiritual gifts for a reason: He has a ministry assignment that He wants you to accomplish in the Body of Christ, a specific job for which He has personally equipped you. God knows whether you are serious about working for Him. If He sees that you just want to discover your gift for the fun of it or because it is the "in thing" to do or because it gives you some new status, you cannot expect Him to help you do it.

If, however, you promise to use your spiritual gift for the glory of God and for the welfare of the Body of Christ, He will help you. Recognize that this is God's best for you. Be open to what He wants to do through you. Discovering gifts is not an ego trip, although it will raise your self-esteem tremendously. If you are ready for a life as an active, productive Christian, you are ready for the five steps. They will help you move into your true destiny.

Fourth, you have to pray. Before, during and after this process you should pray. "If any of you lacks wisdom," James says, "let him ask of God, who gives to all liberally" (Jas. 1:5). Beseech God sincerely and earnestly for His guidance all the way through the five steps. Because God wants you to discover your spiritual gift,

He certainly will give you all the help you need. Just ask and believe that He will. He will give you the revelation that will unlock the beautiful possibilities for the fruitful ministry He has already placed within you.

Knowing these four prerequisites, we are ready for the five steps necessary to discover your spiritual gift.

STEP 1: EXPLORE THE POSSIBILITIES

The first step in planning most human endeavors is to consider all the possible options. If you want to travel from Dallas to Philadelphia, for example, you need to know that it can be done by train, airplane, automobile, motorcycle, horseback, hitchhiking, bus and other ways. If you choose to go by land, you look at a map and explore the various possible routes. Then you choose the one that suits you the best. This is normal and logical.

Likewise, it is difficult to discover a spiritual gift if you do not know approximately what you are looking for ahead of time. The purpose of this first step, explore the possibilities, is to become familiar enough with the different gifts that God ordinarily gives to the Body of Christ so that when you come across your gift later on, you will recognize it for what it really is.

Here are five ways to approach this exciting first step.

Study the Bible

Naturally, the basic source of data about the possible spiritual gifts is located in the Bible. Read the major passages on spiritual gifts time and again. Read them in several different versions. Find examples in the lives of good people in the Bible and how these gifts might have worked in practice. Using whatever helps are available, cross-check Scripture references until you feel you are familiar with what they reveal. Check out the glossary of spiritual gifts in the back of this book and read the Scripture references there.

Learn Your Church's Position on Gifts

As I have mentioned several times, by no means is there universal agreement among churches and denominations about which gifts are in operation today. Nor would I expect these differences to be resolved in our generation.

Because I believe strongly in commitment to the Body of Christ, I believe that when a person voluntarily joins a church, he or she ought to be under the discipline and authority of that church. On the matter of spiritual gifts, the major difference between churches today frequently concerns what I have referred to as the "sign gifts"—mainly speaking in tongues but others as well. Some churches expect the gift of tongues to be used in their worship services. Some have special services on a weekday when tongues can be used, but they do not allow it in Sunday worship. Some do not allow tongues to be used at all at meetings held in the church, but they do not object to it in home cell groups or in private prayer. Other churches are convinced that tongues should not be used at all in our day and age.

Suppose you learn the position of your church on this and other gifts, but you disagree? I suggest one of two courses of action: Either decide to be loyal to your church and its belief and practice without grumbling, or respectfully leave and ask God to take you to another church where you will feel more at home.

At the end of the day, I think God is probably pleased with the variety of gift-mixes being used among the churches and denominations. We need to recognize we are the way we are, individually and collectively, largely because God has made us that way. He gives some of His servants two talents and some five, but He expects us to use all of them to accomplish the Master's purpose.

Read Extensively

Never before have Christian readers had available a richer literary fare on the subject of spiritual gifts. I recommend my more comprehensive work *Your Spiritual Gifts Can Help Your Church Grow* because it includes detailed descriptions of each one of the spiritual gifts. Read other books. List the points where the authors agree on the definition of a particular gift and where they disagree. Put all that together with what you are learning from the Bible and formulate your own opinion. What difference does it really make if I think a certain person's gift is the gift of prophecy and someone else thinks it is knowledge? God is overseeing the whole issue, and He is probably more broad-minded and more flexible than we think. In most cases, He can use us for His glory just the way we are.

Get to Know Gifted People

Seek out and talk to Christian people who have discovered, developed and are using their spiritual gift or gifts. Find out how they articulate what their gifts are and how they interpret their ministry through gifts.

Make Gifts a Conversation Piece

Contemporary Christians have come a long way in understanding spiritual gifts, but even so, a large number are still reluctant to talk about them to each other with ease. An attitude exists that "If I talk about my spiritual gift, people will think I am bragging"; or "If I talk about not having a gift, it's a cop-out." I hope we will shed such inhibitions soon and that we will be able to share openly with each other what our gifts are or what they are not. This will help us and our friends and our children to know what the optimum possibilities are for their ministry.

STEP 2: EXPERIMENT WITH AS MANY GIFTS AS YOU CAN

You would never know you had a talent for bowling, for example, if you had not tried it. You would never know you could write poetry if you had never written some. I wonder if I have a talent for hang gliding? I will never know for sure unless I try it.

Obviously, some spiritual gifts do not lend themselves easily to experimentation. I do not know how to suggest an experiment with the gift of martyrdom, for example. Someone said that that is the gift you only use once! Although some gifts are like that, the majority are not. You can readily experiment with them, and I recommend that you do as much experimenting as possible.

Looking for the Needs

A starting point is to look around and see what needs you can identify. Then try to do something to meet a need. Look for the needs of other people. Look for the needs of the church. Find out where you can be useful in any way, and do it.

Be available for any job around the church you might be asked to do. When you get an assignment, undertake it in prayer. Ask the Lord to show you through that experience whether you might have a spiritual gift along those lines. Hang in there and work hard. Discovering gifts does not usually come quickly. Give each job a fair shake and do not give up easily.

While you are experimenting with the gifts, it is just as important to answer the question, *Which gifts* don't *I have?* as it is to answer the opposite question, *Which gifts* do *I have?* Every gift you find you do *not* have reduces the number of options you need to work at for getting the positive answer.

Let me tell a story which will highlight how important it is to discover, through experimenting, what gift you do *not* have.

When I graduated from Fuller Seminary back in the mid-1950s, I had learned next to nothing about spiritual gifts. I think evangelical leaders generally were still unsure of the Pentecostal movement at that time and had not yet articulated their own position on the gifts. In those days, we certainly were not taught that we had gifts and needed to discover, develop and use them. After seminary, I was ordained by an evangelical Bible-believing church, but not one of the seven ministers on my ordaining council asked me if I had any spiritual gifts or if I knew what they were. I was accepted and served under two evangelical mission agencies. Neither one asked questions about spiritual gifts on their application forms. So I went to Bolivia in 1956 being ignorant of spiritual gifts.

Becoming the Billy Graham of Bolivia?

While I did not know much about spiritual gifts, I did know what I wanted to be. Those were the days when Billy Graham had just moved into orbit. He became the hero of many seminary students, including me. I marveled at the way he would preach to a stadium full of people, deliver a simple Bible message, give an invitation and see people get up all over the place, fill the aisles and pour down to the front to make a decision for Christ. That was for me! My friends and I would imitate Billy Graham's gestures in our preaching classes. We would hold our Bibles like Billy Graham did. We would try to preach with a North Carolina accent. We learned to articulate "The Bible says . . . " and have appropriate sparks of fire in our eyes.

By the time I was ready to go to the mission field, I had it all figured out. Billy Graham could have America—I would take Bolivia! In my mind, I could see thousands and thousands of Bolivians finding Christ through my messages.

I had to spend some time learning Spanish, of course, but when I did, I was ready to begin. I prepared a beautiful sermon in Spanish and used all the homiletical skills I had learned in seminary. I thought the sermon also had one or two things in it that Billy Graham himself might not have thought of. Then I preached the sermon with all my heart and gave the invitation. Nobody came!

Disappointed and somewhat dejected, I tried to figure out what had happened. Perhaps it had to do with prayer. Even at best I have never been a great prayer warrior, but with all the effort it took me to prepare the sermon that time, I had to admit I had hardly prayed at all. So I prepared another sermon using the best principles of homiletics. But this time I prayed intensely before I went into the pulpit. The results were the same. Nobody came. People acted as if they were permanently glued to their seats.

I then thought something in my life must be blocking my relationship with the Lord. The consecration theology I was taught had programmed me to feel that I must not properly be "presenting my body as a living sacrifice," for if I were doing that, certainly God would bless my evangelistic ministry.

My thoughts went back to seminary again. I recalled a professor of personal evangelism who used to keep our class spellbound by telling stories of how God had used him to win others to Christ. He would tell about how he would get on a bus and sit next to a total stranger, and by the time they got off the bus the stranger would have accepted Christ. I was impressed!

So I got on a bus and took a seat next to a total stranger. By the time we got off the bus, he was mad at me! I was devastated!

For months and years during that first term of missionary service I went through experience after experience like that. I wanted to be Bolivia's Billy Graham, but something was preventing me from doing it.

Making the Most Important Discovery

Then, little by little, I finally began to learn about spiritual gifts. As I matured in that process, one day I made what I now consider one of the most important spiritual discoveries of my Christian life—*God had not given me the gift of evangelist!*

From that day on, I have been a better Christian, a better missionary, a more joyous person, a better husband and father and a more competent servant of God. When I realized that on the Day of Judgment, God is not going to hold me accountable for what I did as an evangelist, I felt liberated. Guilt rolled off like the load on the back of Christian in *Pilgrim's Progress*. It was God Himself who had never wanted me to be the Billy Graham of Bolivia. What a relief!

I had experimented with a spiritual gift. I had tried hard to use it. And I had come to the important discovery that I did not have the gift.

Let me hasten to say that although I may not have the *gift* of evangelist, like every other Christian I do have a *role* of witness. Wherever I go and at all times I try to be a good representative of God. I know how to share Christ, and I occasionally lead people to the Lord. Not having the gift of evangelist should never be a cop-out from our responsibility of consistent witnessing for Christ.

Using the Gifts Inventories

One of the best ways to determine which gifts to experiment with first is to go through the spiritual-gifts questionnaire found in chapter 7. Although a gifts inventory like this should not be considered the final word on discovering gifts, it can be very helpful in pointing you in the right direction. This questionnaire scores each gift from 0 to 15, and I suggest that you begin seriously experimenting with, say, the top 3 or 4.

As you do, don't forget to ask yourself two questions: (1) *Do I have it?* and (2) *Don't I have it?*

Step 3: Examine Your Feelings

Somewhere along the line, personal feelings have fallen into disrepute with many believers. If a person is found really enjoying life, according to this way of thinking, something must be wrong. But, happily, things are changing. The new teaching on spiritual gifts is opening the way for an age in which serving God can be fun.

My concept is this: The same God who gives spiritual gifts also oversees the way each one of us is made up in our total being. God knows every detail of our psychological condition, our glands and hormones, our metabolism, our total personality. He understands our feelings perfectly. He knows our personality profile. And He also knows that if we enjoy doing a task, we do a better job at it than if we do not enjoy it. So part of God's plan, as I understand it, is to match the spiritual gift He gives us with our temperament in such a way that if we really have a gift, we will feel good using it. I think that this is why God reserves the assigning of spiritual gifts for Himself. All the computers at IBM would not be equipped to assign gifts to the hundreds of millions of Christians around the world, but it is no problem to God Almighty.

The Bible also tells us that this is the way God wants to lead His people. Psalm 37:4 says, "Delight yourself also in the LORD, and He shall give you the desires of your heart." Philippians 2:13 adds, "For it is God who works in you both to will and to do for His good pleasure." Apparently, when people are doing God's will, they will be doing what they *want* to do because God has given them that desire. Biblically, then, it is clear that we should not have a conflict between enjoying ourselves and pleasing God.

Why Peter Wagner Is Not Your Pastor!

During that same first term as a missionary when I discovered I did not have the gift of evangelist, I also discovered, largely through feelings this time, that I did not have the gift of pastor.

We were assigned by our mission to the small village of San José de Chiquitos where, among other things, we were to plant a new church. We started the church, small and struggling as it was. But in the course of trying out pastoral work, I learned I was not well equipped to handle people's personal problems. When someone begins to tell me about his or her personal life, I come unglued. I tend to worry about it, lose sleep over it, want to cry and overreact in many ways. I make all the wrong moves. I cannot trust my intuitions. In short, my feelings tell me God has not given me the pastor gift.

Of course, I do have the role of occasionally helping others through their problems and relating in a pastoral way when certain situations occur. Members of my family, certain friends and, at times, students need my help, and I try to give it to them as best I can. My rate of success at personal counseling is extremely low, somewhere near zero. And because I react so poorly, I tend to avoid counseling situations as much as possible. Some find it hard to understand that listening to other people's problems can be a drain on emotional energies for those of us who do not have the gift of pastor.

Even after I had realized that I do not have the gift of pastor, I did accept a pastorate once. An important principle lay behind my acceptance. Sometimes a circumstance will arise when we take on a responsibility for a season simply because it is the right thing to do, not because we necessarily have a gift for it. In my case it meant filling in as pastor of a large city church in Bolivia during the time when the pastor took a year's leave of absence in order to coordinate a massive nationwide evangelistic initiative. At that point I was willing to do what I was called upon to do, although it meant ministering for a time on the basis of a role rather than a gift.

How God Works Within Each of Us

I had been teaching this step about testing your feelings for several years, when a wonderful confirmation came. It turned out that Peyton Marshall, a graduate student in psychology at St. Louis University, did his doctoral dissertation on spiritual gifts.

He compared the results of testing people with the Wagner-Modified Houts Questionnaire (the one found in chapter 7 of this book) and the famous Myers-Briggs psychological test. Marshall found that he could predict how a person would score on my questionnaire by how that person scored on Myers-Briggs. With that, there's no reason to doubt that God matches the gifts He gives us to our temperment and our personality.

Although feelings may have to be put aside from time to time on the basis of a situation like pastoring that church in Bolivia, it should only be temporary. The normal thing is for Christians to feel excited about the work they are doing for God because they have discovered the spiritual gift or gifts that God has given them. While experimenting with the gifts, then, it is important to examine your feelings.

STEP 4: EVALUATE YOUR EFFECTIVENESS

Since spiritual gifts are task oriented toward doing ministry, it is not out of order to expect them to work. If God has given you a gift, He has done so because He wants you to accomplish something for Him in the context of the Body of Christ. Gifted people see results for their efforts. Postulating that God wants us to be successful is not contradictory to sincere Christian humility. If you experiment with a gift and consistently find that what it is supposed to accomplish does not happen, you probably have discovered another one of the gifts God has not given you.

This is where I got my first clues that I do not have the gift of evangelist. I tried with dedication and sincerity and it simply did not work. I tried public evangelism and I failed. I tried personal evangelism and got knots in my stomach and became tongue-tied. I kept trying to witness to people next to me on airplanes and I can't remember one whom I succeeded in leading to Christ.

When I observed some of my friends who were effortlessly witnessing and leading large numbers of people to Christ, I then knew that, compared to them, I was getting very little supernatural help in evangelizing. It was the flesh, not the Spirit. God was trying to tell me something.

On the other hand, a major reason that I know I have the gift of teaching is that people learn when I teach, whether in classrooms or through my books. I have a high expectation that if you have read this book up to here, you have learned something that you didn't know previously—even if you have read another of my books on spiritual gifts or heard me teach a lesson on the subject. I am not saying this to boast; I am saying it only to point out that the Holy Spirit gives me supernatural help when I teach. I do not detect this kind of help when I attempt to evangelize.

If you have the gift of evangelist, people will come to Christ regularly through your ministry. You will love to evangelize. If you have the gift of exhortation, you will help people through their problems and see many lives straightened out. If you have the gift of healing, sick people will consistently get well. If you have the gift of administration, the organization will run smoothly. When true gifts are in operation, whatever is supposed to happen through them will happen.

STEP 5: EXPECT CONFIRMATION FROM THE BODY

If you think you have a spiritual gift and you have been trying your best to exercise it but if no one else in your church thinks you have it, you probably do not. A gift needs to be confirmed.

At this point, you might sense a conflict between step 4 concerning your feelings and step 5 concerning confirmation. Feelings are important, but they are far from infallible. You may have a deep desire to help other people, for example. You may feel strongly that God is calling you to minister through counseling or through the gift of exhortation. But if you have been experimenting with counseling and have found that over a period of time very few people seek you out for help or recommend their friends and relatives to you or write notes to you telling how much you have helped them, you have good reason to doubt the validity of your feelings as far as that spiritual gift is concerned. Confirmation from the Body serves as a check on all the other steps. Although I have listed this step last, in some ways it can be the most important of all.

The gifts, according to our definition, are given for use within the context of the Body. It is necessary, then, that other members of the Body have an important say in confirming your gift.

Another reason why confirmation from the Body is so important is that it builds in a system of accountability for the use of gifts. Whereas it is true that we are ultimately accountable to God, more immediately we are accountable to each other and we need to take this seriously. In the Church we need to act like a team. We need the other players and they need us. Our goals are not individual goals, they are goals of the team.

If you have the gift of administration or helps or hospitality or mercy but nobody else knows it, you may easily fall into the trap of being lazy about using it, thinking that no one will know the difference. But once your gift is known and confirmed by the Body, your friends will rightly expect to see it in action. This is why I pointed out earlier that a desire to work hard is a prerequisite for discovering spiritual gifts. When members of the Body confirm one another's gifts, more can be accomplished just on the basis of people working harder at what God has called them to do, and the Church will be healthy.

For some years, I thought I had the gift of administration. Somewhat against my will at first, I was talked into taking over the administration of the mission agency under which we were serving. As I experimented with administration, I began to enjoy it quite a bit. As far as feelings were concerned, it seemed like it might be a gift. Then when my position would come up for confirmation at the annual field conference meeting, a good bit of disagreement would occur among fellow workers about whether I was the right person for the job. Whenever the vote came, I would barely squeak by. Looking back I now realize that I needed someone who had the gift of exhortation to tell me to get out of administration and go back to teaching, but either that person was not there or I was not listening. So I continued for some years and predictably the mission did not advance greatly under my management.

Only after I got back to the United States and read *The Making of a Christian Leader* by my close friend Ted Engstrom did I begin to understand clearly that I never did have the gift of administration. In this case, another member of the Body confirmed to me that I did not have the gift, and I have been grateful to Ted Engstrom ever since. In fact, that became very important when, later on, Fuller Seminary offered me a promotion to a position of administration and I turned it down because I knew that I did not have the gift for it. And as it turned out, I was much happier teaching.

FIND YOUR SPIRITUAL GIFT!

This chapter has been so autobiographical that an explanation might be in order. As many evangelists have discovered, personal testimonies can be extremely helpful in motivating people, because they provide something of flesh and blood with which to identify. Abstract concepts are fine, but they rarely move people. My purpose in this chapter has been to help you see more clearly how you can begin the exciting process of discovering your spiritual gift or gifts.

Let me give a final example of how it can work by quoting a letter from one of the most successful church-growth pastors in the United Methodist Church, Joe Harding. At the time of this incident, Pastor Harding's church, the Central United Protestant Church of Richland, Washington, was one of the largest and fastest-growing churches of the whole Northwest, an area not particularly known for explosive church growth. Joe Harding had enrolled in a church-growth seminar, which I was teaching in Harding's own church facilities. A few days after I taught my lesson on spiritual gifts, Joe wrote me this letter:

> Your class was particularly helpful to me in making a major decision. Just a few days before the class I had received a telephone call from one of our denominational executives asking me to move to a national office in the Board of Discipleship in Nashville to head up a new program of evangelism. I was told that I was their first choice and they really wanted me to accept this responsibility. I am acquainted with the program and I am enthusiastic about it.
>
> However, as I weighed the matter very carefully it was clear to me that my gifts are not primarily in administration, but in preaching and teaching and in pastoring. When I measured my personal gifts against the requirements of this challenging job, it was very easy for me to decline and to feel that God was calling me to remain in this congregation to demonstrate the potential of dynamic and vital growth within the Methodist church.
>
> I was in agony when I first received the call, because I felt I could not decline such a challenging opportunity. Your emphasis on the joy that you find in exercising the gifts put the matter in an entirely different perspective. I find that tremendous joy in standing before the

congregation that I preach to, Sunday after Sunday. I simply know that that is what God is calling me to do.

So your class came at a most appropriate time in my life and I simply want to share my gratitude with you.[1]

The thrill I got from receiving Joe Harding's letter could not have been any less than that which Billy Graham must feel when 3,000 people come forward in one of his crusades. I now thank God that I am not the Billy Graham of Bolivia as I once thought I might be. God had something much better for *me*. He has a similar exciting and fulfilling purpose in mind for *you*.

Note

1. Joseph Harding, letter to the author, no date.

CHAPTER 7

Let's Get STARTED!

Are you ready to actually begin to discover what spiritual gifts God has given you for your life and your ministry? This chapter will give you a running start.

BEFORE YOU START

You are now about to become involved in an exciting spiritual exercise. You know that God has given you one or more spiritual gifts, and discovering that gift or gifts will be a thrilling experience.

You will be asked to rate the 125 statements found in the Wagner-Modified Houts Questionnaire. Thousands and thousands of believers have been blessed by taking the Wagner-Modified Houts Questionnaire over the years. Constant feedback from them has enabled me to refine the questionnaire to the point where it will give you a fairly accurate picture of what kind of ministry God expects you to be carrying out in your group of believers.

However, do not regard the results of this test as final. The three or four gifts you score highest in may or may not be your real spiritual gifts. But you can be sure in any case that they are a starting point for prayer and experimentation. You will need other members of the Body of Christ to help you confirm what gifts you have. I have omitted the gift of martrydom from the questionnaire because, after considerable experimentation, I could not find a valid way to test for it.

Also, please remember that when I created this questionnaire, I had not yet discovered the gifts of apostle and leading worship (music). For this reason, you will not find them reflected in the questions, nor in the analysis that follows. Unfortunately the Wagner-Modified Houts Questionnaire, which is well known and widely used in its original form, cannot be changed at this point. But keeping in mind that the general rule that the results of this test are neither final nor definitive will put this in perspective.

WHEN YOU'RE READY

With that caveat, let's begin:

- **Step 1.** Go through the list of 125 statements in the questionnaire. For each one, mark to what extent the statement has been true of your life: Much, Some, Little or Not at All. **Warning!** Do not score according to what you think should be true of your life or what you hope might be true in the future. Be honest and score each question on the basis of actual past experience.
- **Step 2.** When you are finished, calculate your score by means of the Scoring Chart. Go back through your 125 answers and give yourself 3 points for "Much"; 2 points for "Some"; 1 point for "Little"; and 0 for "Not at All." Then add up the total for each of the rows A through Y. You will immediately see which gifts are strongest and which are weakest. Compare your score with the definitions in the glossary.
- **Step 3.** Finally, complete the exercises in Step 3: Gifts and Ministries Analysis to gain a preliminary evalua-

tion of where your gifts may lie. Explore with friends the implications this might have for your ongoing ministry in the Body of Christ.

STEP 1: WAGNER-MODIFIED HOUTS QUESTIONNAIRE

For each statement, mark to what extent it is true of your life: **M**uch, **S**ome, **L**ittle or **N**ot at All.

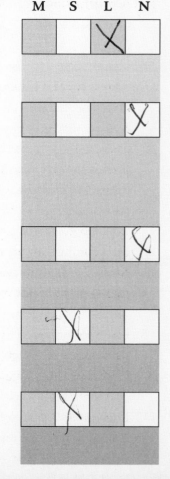

	M	S	L	N
1. I have a desire to speak direct messages from God that edify, exhort or comfort others.			X	
2. I have enjoyed relating to a certain group of people over a long period of time, sharing personally in their successes and failures.				X
3. People have told me that I helped them learn biblical truth in a meaningful way.				X
4. I have applied spiritual truth effectively to situations in my own life.		X		
5. Others have told me that I helped them distinguish key and important facts of Scripture.		X		

	M	S	L	N

6. I have verbally encouraged the wavering, the troubled or the discouraged. [M: X]

7. Others in the church have noted that I was able to see through phoniness before it was evident to other people. [M: X]

8. I find I manage money well in order to give liberally to the Lord's work. [M: X]

9. I have assisted Christian leaders to relieve them for their essential job. [N: X]

10. I have a desire to work with those who have physical or mental problems, to alleviate their suffering. [N: X]

11. I feel comfortable relating to ethnics and minorities, and they seem to accept me. [L: X]

12. I have led others to a decision for salvation through faith in Christ. [L: X]

13. My home is always open to people passing through who need a place to stay. [N: X]

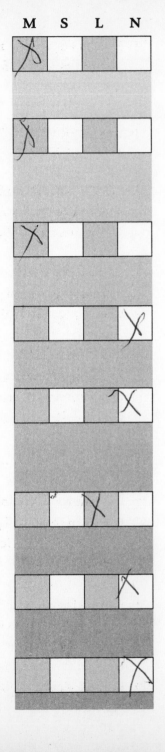

	M	S	L	N

14. When in a group, I am the one others look to for vision and direction.

15. When I speak, people seem to listen and agree.

16. When a group I am in is lacking organization, I tend to step in and fill the gap.

17. Others can point to specific instances where my prayers have resulted in visible miracles.

18. In the name of the Lord, I have been used in curing diseases instantaneously.

19. I have spoken in tongues.

20. Sometimes when I person speaks in tongues, I get ideas about what God is saying.

21. I could live more comfortably, but I choose not to in order to live with the poor.

22. I am single and enjoy it.

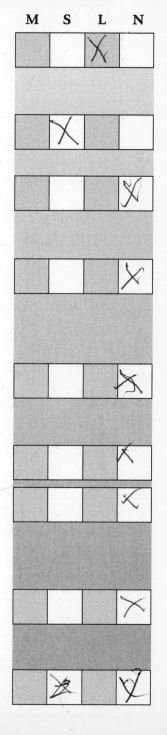

	M	S	L	N
23. I spend at least an hour a day in prayer.				X
24. I have spoken to evil spirits and they have obeyed me.				X
25. I enjoy being called upon to do special jobs around the church.				X
26. Through God I have revealed specific things that will happen in the future.				X
27. I have enjoyed assuming the responsibility for the spiritual well-being of a particular group of Christians.				X
28. I feel I can explain the New Testament teaching about the health and ministry of the Body of Christ in a relevant way.				X
29. I can intuitively arrive at solutions to fairly complicated problems.		X		
30. I have had insights of spiritual truth that others have said helped bring them closer to God.			X	X

	M	S	L	N

31. I can effectively motivate people to get involved in ministry when it is needed.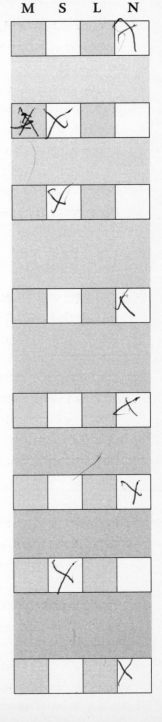

32. From time to time, I can "see" the Spirit of God resting on certain people.

33. My giving records show that I give considerably more than 10 percent of my income to the Lord's work.

34. Other people have told me that I have helped them become more effective in their ministries.

35. I have cared for others when they have had material or physical needs.

36. I feel I could learn another language well in order to minister to those in a different culture.

37. I have shared joyfully how Christ has brought me to Himself in a way that is meaningful to nonbelievers.

38. I enjoy taking charge of church suppers or social events.

	M	S	L	N

39. I have believed God for the impossible and seen it happen in a tangible way.

| | X | | |

40. Other Christians have followed my leadership because they believed in me.

| | | | X |

41. I enjoy handling the details of organizing ideas, people, resources and time for more effective ministry.

| | | | X |

42. God has used me personally to perform supernatural signs and wonders.

| | | | X |

43. I enjoy praying for sick people because I know that many of them will be healed as a result.

| | | | X |

44. I have spoken an immediate message of God to His people in a language I have never learned.

| | | | X |

45. I have interpreted tongues with the result that the Body of Christ was edified, exhorted or comforted.

| | | | X |

46. Living a simple lifestyle is an exciting challenge for me.

| | | X | X |

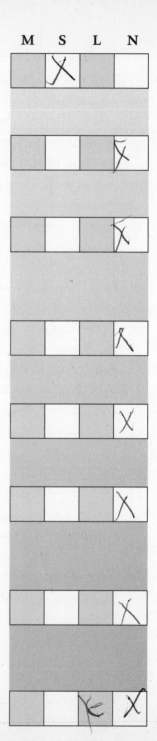

M   S   L   N

47. Other people have noted that I feel more indifferent about not being married than most.

48. When I hear a prayer request, I pray for that need for several days at least.

49. I have actually heard a demon speak in a loud voice.

50. I don't have many special skills, but I do what needs to be done around the church.

51. People have told me that I have communicated timely and urgent messages which must have come directly from the Lord.

52. I feel unafraid of giving spiritual guidance and direction in a group of Christians.

53. I can devote considerable time to learning new biblical truths in order to communicate them to others.

54. When a person has a problem, I can frequently guide them to the best biblical solution.

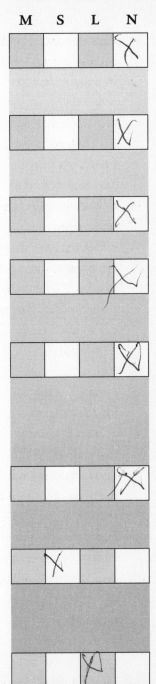

	M	S	L	N

55. Through study or experience I have discerned major strategies or techniques God seems to use in furthering His kingdom.

56. People have come to me in their afflictions or suffering and have told me that they have been helped, relieved and healed.

57. I can tell with a fairly high degree of assurance when a person is afflicted by an evil spirit.

58. When I am moved by an appeal to give to God's work, I usually find the money I need to do it.

59. I have enjoyed doing routine tasks that led to more effective ministry by others.

60. I enjoy visiting in hospitals and/or retirement homes, and I feel I do well in such a ministry.

61. People of a different race or culture have been attracted to me, and we have related well.

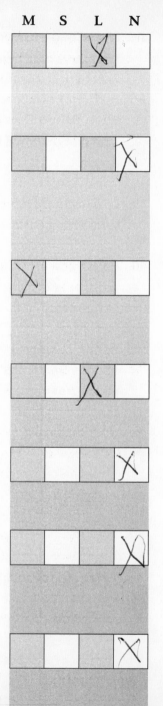

	M	S	L	N

62. Non-Christians have noted that they feel comfortable when they are around me and that I have a positive effect on them toward developing a faith in Christ.

63. When people come to my home, they indicate that they "feel at home" with me.

64. Other people have told me that I have faith to accomplish what seemed impossible to them.

65. When I set goals, others seem to accept them readily.

66. I have been able to make effective and efficient plans for accomplishing the goals of a group.

67. God regularly seems to do impossible things through my life.

68. Others have told me that God healed them of an emotional problem when I ministered to them.

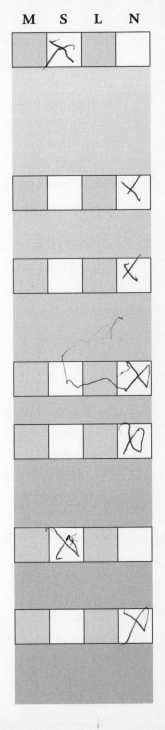

	M	S	L	N
69. I can speak to God in a lan- guage I have never learned.				X
70. I have prayed that I may inter- pret if someone begins speak- ing in tongues.				X
71. I am not poor, but I can iden- tify with poor people.			X	X
72. I am glad I have more time to serve the Lord because I am single.				X
73. Intercessory prayer is one of my favorite ways of spending time.				X
74. Others call on me when they suspect that someone is demonized.				X
75. Others have mentioned that I seem to enjoy routine tasks and do well at them.				X
76. I sometimes have a strong sense of what God wants to say to people in response to a particular situation.		X		
77. I have helped fellow believers by guiding them to relevant		X		

M S L N

portions of the Bible and praying for them.

78. I feel I can communicate biblical truths to others and see
resulting changes in knowledge, attitudes, values or
conduct.

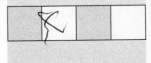

79. Some people indicate that
I have perceived and applied
biblical truth to the specific
needs of fellow believers.

80. I study and read quite a bit
in order to learn new biblical
truths.

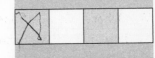

81. I have a desire to effectively
counsel the perplexed, the
guilty and the addicted.

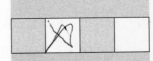

82. I can recognize whether a
person's teaching is from
God, from Satan or of
human origin.

83. I am so confident that God
will meet my needs that I give
to Him sacrificially and
consistently.

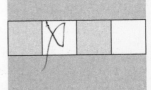

	M	S	L	N

84. When I do things behind the scenes and others are helped, I am joyful. — **M**

85. People call on me to help those who are less fortunate. — **N**

86. I would be willing to leave comfortable surroundings if it would enable me to share Christ with more people. — **S**

87. I get frustrated when others don't seem to share their faith with nonbelievers as much as I do. — **N**

88. Others have mentioned to me that I am a very hospitable person. — **N**

89. There have been times when I have felt sure that I knew God's specific will for the future growth of His work, even when others have not been so sure. — **L**

90. When I join a group, others seem to back off and expect me to take the leadership. — **N**

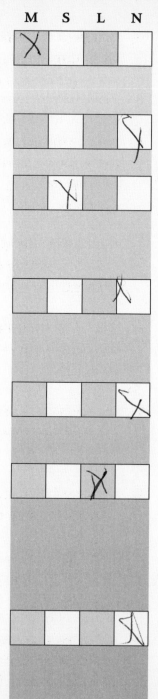

	M	S	L	N

91. I am able to give directions to others without using persuasion to get them to accomplish a task.

92. People have told me that I was God's instrument that brought supernatural change in lives or circumstances.

93. I have prayed for others and physical healing has actually occurred.

94. When I give a public message in tongues, I expect it to be interpreted.

95. I have interpreted tongues in a way that seemed to bless others.

96. Others tell me I sacrifice much materially in order to minister.

97. I am single and have little difficulty controlling my sexual desires.

98. Others have told me that my prayers for them have been answered in tangible ways.

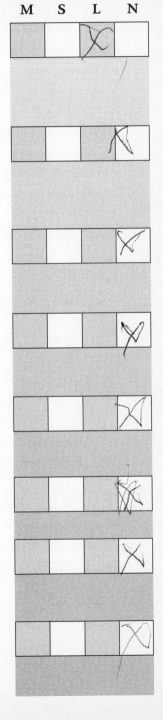

	M	S	L	N

99. Other people have been instantly delivered from demonic oppression when I have prayed for them. — N

100. I prefer being active and doing something, rather than just sitting around talking, reading or listening to a speaker. — L

101. I sometimes feel that I know exactly what God wants to do in ministry at a specific point in time. — L

102. People have told me that I have helped them be restored to the Christian community. — N

103. Studying the Bible and sharing my insights with others is very satisfying for me. — M

104. I have felt an unusual presence of God and personal confidence when important decisions needed to be made. — S

105. I have the ability to discover new truths for myself through reading or observing situations first-hand. — M

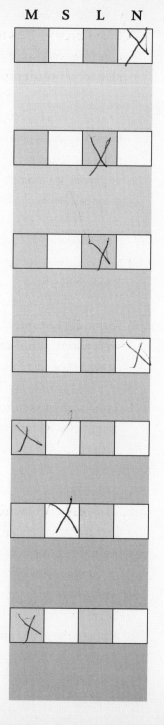

	M	S	L	N

106. I have urged others to seek a biblical solution to their affliction or suffering.

107. I can tell whether a person speaking in tongues is genuine.

108. I have been willing to maintain a lower standard of living in order to benefit God's work.

109. When I serve the Lord, I really don't care who gets the credit.

110. I would enjoy spending time with a lonely shut-in person or someone in prison.

111. More than most, I have had a strong desire to see peoples of other countries won to the Lord.

112. I am attracted to nonbelievers because of my desire to win them to Christ.

113. I have desired to make my home available to those in the Lord's service whenever needed.

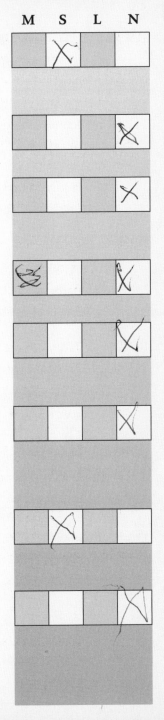

	M	S	L	N
114. Others have told me that I am a person of unusual vision, and I agree.	X			
115. When I am in charge, things seem to run smoothly.				X
116. I have enjoyed bearing the responsibility for the success of a particular task within my church.				X
117. In the name of the Lord, I have been able to give sight to the blind.			X	
118. When I pray for the sick, either I or they feel sensations of tingling or warmth.				X
119. When I speak in tongues, I believe it is edifying to the Body of Christ.				X
120. I have interpreted tongues in such a way that the message appeared to be directly from God.				X
121. Poor people accept me because I choose to live on their level.				X

	M	S	L	N
122. I readily identify with Paul's desire for others to be single as he was.				X
123. When I pray, God frequently speaks to me, and I recognize His voice.			X	
124. I cast out demons in Jesus' name.				X
125. I respond cheerfully when asked to do a job, even if it seems menial.		X		

STEP 2: SCORING CHART

In the grid below, enter the numerical value of each of your responses next to the number of the corresponding statements from Step 1.

MUCH=3   SOME=2   LITTLE=1   NOT AT ALL=0

Then add up the five numbers that you have recorded in each row and place the sum in the Total column.

Row		Value of Answers									Total	Gift (see chapter 3)
A	1		26		51		76		101			Prophecy
B	2		27		52		77		102			Pastor
C	3		28		53		78		103			Teaching
D	4		29		54		79		104			Wisdom
E	5		30		55		80		105			Knowledge
F	6		31		56		81		106			Exhortation
G	7		32		57		82		107			Discerning of spirits
H	8		33		58		83		108			Giving
I	9		34		59		84		109			Helps
J	10		35		60		85		110			Mercy
K	11		36		61		86		111			Missionary
L	12		37		62		87		112			Evangelist
M	13		38		63		88		113			Hospitality
N	14		39		64		89		114			Faith
O	15		40		65		90		115			Leadership
P	16		41		66		91		116			Administration
Q	17		42		67		92		117			Miracles
R	18		43		68		93		118			Healing
S	19		44		69		94		119			Tongues
T	20		45		70		95		120			Interpre. of tongues
U	21		46		71		96		121			Voluntary poverty
V	22		47		72		97		122			Celibacy
W	23		48		73		98		123			Intercession
X	24		49		74		99		124			Deliverance
Y	25		50		75		100		125			Service

STEP 3: GIFTS AND MINISTRIES ANALYSIS

1. Using the results of the Scoring Chart on p. 88, enter below in the "Dominant" section your three highest-rated gifts. Then enter in the "Subordinate" section the next three highest-scoring gifts. This will give you a *tentative* evaluation of where your gifts may lie.

Dominant:

1. _Discerning of Spirits_

2. _~~Wisdom~~ Faith_

3. _~~Giving~~ Prophecy_

Subordinate: *Wisdom*

1. _~~Knowledge~~_

2. _~~Teaching~~ Exhortation_ *Knowledge Giving*

3. _~~Exhortation~~, Faith_

2. What ministries are you now performing (formally or informally) in the Body?

~~Discerning~~   _____

~~Giving~~   _____

~~Teaching~~   _____

3. Are there any of these ministries that you are not especially gifted for? God may be calling you to consider changes.

_____

_____

_____

4. Is your vocational status lay or clergy?

_____

5. In light of your gift cluster and vocational status, what are some ministry models or roles suitable for you? What specific roles in the Body of Christ has God possibly gifted you for?

_____   _____

_____   _____

_____   _____

GLOSSARY

of Spiritual GIFTS

Administration: The special ability to understand clearly the immediate and long-range goals of a particular unit of the Body and to devise and execute effective plans for the accomplishment of those goals (see Luke 14:28-30; Acts 6:1-7; 27:11; 1 Cor. 12:28; Titus 1:5).

Apostle: The special ability to assume and exercise general leadership within God-assigned spheres such as ecclesiastical, territorial, functional, marketplace, etc., accompanied by an extraordinary authority in spiritual matters that is spontaneously recognized and appreciated by those within the sphere (see 1 Cor. 12:28; Eph. 2:20; 4:11).

Celibacy: The special ability to remain single and enjoy it and not suffer undue sexual temptations (see Matt. 19:10-12; 1 Cor. 7:7-8).

Deliverance: The special ability to cast out demons and evil spirits (see Matt. 12:22-32; Luke 10:12-20; Acts 8:5-8; 16:16-18).

Discerning of spirits: The special ability to know with assurance whether certain behaviors purported to be of God are in reality divine, human or satanic (see Matt. 16:21-23; Acts 5:1-11; 16:16-18; 1 Cor. 12:10; 1 John 4:1-6).

Evangelist: The special ability to share the gospel with unbelievers in such a way that men and women become Jesus' disciples and responsible members of the Body of Christ (see Acts 8:5-6,26-40; 14:21; 21:8; Eph. 4:11-14; 2 Tim. 4:5).

Exhortation: The special ability to minister words of comfort, consolation, encouragement and counsel to other members of the Body in such a way that they feel helped and healed (see Acts 14:22; Rom. 12:8; 1 Tim. 4:13; Heb. 10:25).

Faith: The special ability to discern with extraordinary confidence the will and purposes of God for the future of His work (see Acts 11:22-24; 27:21-25; Rom. 4:18-21; 1 Cor. 12:9; Heb. 11).

Giving: The special ability to contribute their material resources to the work of the Lord with liberality and cheerfulness (see Mark 12:41-44; Rom. 12:8; 2 Cor. 8:1-7; 9:2-8).

Healing: The special ability to serve as human intermediaries through whom it pleases God to cure illness and restore health apart from the use of natural means (see Acts 3:1-10; 5:12-16; 9:32-35; 28:7-10; 1 Cor. 12:9,28).

Helps: The special ability to invest their talents in the life and ministry of other members of the Body, most frequently leaders, thus enabling the leader to increase the effectiveness of his or her spiritual gifts (see Mark 15:40-41; Luke 8:2-3; Acts 9:36; Rom. 16:1-2; 1 Cor. 12:28).

Hospitality: The special ability to provide an open house and warm welcome for those in need of food and lodging (see Acts 16:14-15; Rom. 12:9-13; 16:23; Heb. 13:1-2; 1 Pet. 4:9).

Intercession: The special ability to pray for extended periods of time on a regular basis and see frequent and specific answers to their prayers to a degree much greater than that which is expected of the average Christian (see Luke 22:41-44; Acts 12:12; Col. 1:9-12; 4:12-13; 1 Tim. 2:1-2; Jas. 5:14-16).

Interpretation of tongues: The special ability to make known in the vernacular the message of one who speaks in tongues (see 1 Cor. 12:10,30; 14:13-14,26-28).

Knowledge: The special ability to discover, accumulate, analyze and clarify information and ideas that are pertinent to the growth and well-being of the Body (see Acts 5:1-11; 1 Cor. 2:14; 12:8; 2 Cor. 11:6; Col. 2:2-3).

Leadership: The special ability to set goals in accordance with God's purpose for the future and to communicate these goals to others in such a way that they voluntarily and harmoniously work together to accomplish those goals for the glory of God (see Luke 9:51; Acts 7:10; 15:7-11; Rom. 12:8; 1 Tim. 5:17; Heb. 13:17).

Leading worship: The special ability to usher a congregation into the presence of God through music, prayer, dance and other visual forms (see 1 Sam. 16:23; 1 Chron. 9:33; Ps. 34:3).

Martyrdom: The special ability to undergo suffering for the faith even to death while consistently displaying a joyous and victorious attitude that brings glory to God (see Acts 22:20; 1 Cor. 13:3; Rev. 2:13; 17:6).

Mercy: The special ability to feel genuine empathy and compassion for individuals, both Christian and non-Christian, who suffer distressing physical, mental or emotional problems, and to translate that compassion into cheerfully done deeds that reflect Christ's love and alleviate the suffering (see Matt. 20:29-34; 25:34-40; Mark 9:41; Luke 10:33-35; Acts 11:28-30; 16:33-34; Rom. 12:8).

Miracles: The special ability to serve as human intermediaries through whom it pleases God to perform powerful acts that are perceived by observers to have altered the ordinary course of nature (see Acts 9:36-42; 19:11-20; 20:7-12; Rom. 15:18-19; 1 Cor. 12:10,28; 2 Cor. 12:12).

Missionary: The special ability to minister in another culture other spiritual gifts (see Acts 8:4; 13:2-3; 22:21; Rom. 10:15; 1 Cor. 9:19-23).

Pastor: The special ability to assume a long-term personal responsibility for the spiritual welfare of a group of believers (see John 10:1-18; Eph. 4:11-14; 1 Tim. 3:1-7; 1 Pet. 5:1-3).

Prophecy: The special ability to receive and communicate an immediate message of God to His people through a divinely anointed utterance (see Luke 7:26; Acts 15:32; Acts 21:9-11; Rom. 12:6; 1 Cor. 12:10,28; Eph. 4:11-13).

Service: The special ability to identify the unmet needs involved in a task related to God's work and to make use of available resources to meet those needs and help accomplish the desired goals (see Acts 6:1-7; Rom. 12:7; Gal. 6:2,10; 2 Tim. 1:16-18; Titus 3:14).

Teaching: The special ability to communicate information relevant to the health and ministry of the Body and its members in such a way that others will learn (see Acts 18:24-28; 20:20-21; Rom. 12:7; 1 Cor. 12:28; Eph. 4:11-14).

Tongues: The special ability (1) to speak to God in a language they have never learned and/or (2) to receive and communicate an immediate message from God to His people through a divinely anointed utterance in a language they have never learned (see Mark 16:17; Acts 2:1-13; 10:44-46; 19:1-7; 1 Cor. 12:10,28; 14:13-19).

Voluntary poverty: The special ability to serve God more effectively by renouncing material comfort and luxury and adopting a personal lifestyle equivalent to those living at the poverty level in a given society (see Acts 2:44-45; 4:34-37; 1 Cor. 13:1-3; 2 Cor. 6:10; 8:9).

Wisdom: The special ability to know the mind of the Holy Spirit in such a way as to receive insight into how given knowledge may best be applied to specific needs arising in the Body of Christ (see Acts 6:3,10; 1 Cor. 2:1-13; 12:8; Jas. 1:5-6; 2 Pet. 3:15-16).

More Life-Changing Reading from C. Peter Wagner

Your Spiritual Gifts Can Help Your Church Grow
How To Find Your Gifts and Use Them To Bless Others
C. Peter Wagner
Trade Paper
ISBN 08307.16815

Finding Your Spiritual Gifts
The Wagner-Modified Houts Spritual Gifts Inventory
C. Peter Wagner
Questionnaire
ISBN 08307.17889

Your Spiritual Gifts Can Help Your Church Grow
(Spiritual Gifts Inventory)
Group Study Guide
C. Peter Wagner
Manual
ISBN 08307.17587

Your Spiritual Gifts Can Help Your Church Grow
Video Study Package
C. Peter Wagner
Video
ISBN 607135.001959

Acts of the Holy Spirit
A Complete Commentary on the Book of Acts
C. Peter Wagner
Paperback
ISBN 08307.20413

Churchquake!
How the Apostolic Reformation Is Shaking Up the Church As We Know It
C. Peter Wagner
Paperback
ISBN 08307.19180